KV-523-849

The authors

Richard Muscat is Professor in Behavioural Neuroscience, Department of Biomedical Sciences at the University of Malta, and Chair of the National Drug Commission in Malta. Within the Pompidou Group he is the co-ordinator of the Research Platform. He wrote the synthesis.

Dirk J. Korf is Professor in Criminology at the Universities of Amsterdam and Utrecht, and Chairperson of the European Society for Social Drug Research (ESSD).

Jorge Negreiros is Professor at the University of Porto, Faculty of Psychology and Education Sciences.

Dominique Vuillaume works at the Joint Ministerial Task Force for Combating Drugs and Drug Addiction (MILDT), Paris.

3033312

Signals from drug research

Richard Muscat

Dirk J. Korf

Jorge Negreiros

Dominique Vuillaume

Council of Europe Publishing

French edition:

Tendances de la recherche sur les drogues

ISBN 978-92-871-6693-7

The opinions expressed in this work are the responsibility of the authors and do not necessarily reflect the official policy of the Council of Europe.

All rights reserved. No part of this publication may be translated, reproduced or transmitted, in any form or by any means, electronic (CD-Rom, Internet, etc.) or mechanical, including photocopying, recording or any information storage or retrieval system, without prior permission in writing from the Public Information and Publications Division, Directorate of Communication (F-67075 Strasbourg Cedex or publishing@coe.int).

UNIVERSITIES AT MEDWAY
2 5 FEB 2011
DRILL HALL LIBRARY

Cover illustration: © Sara Whomsley
Cover design and layout: Documents and Publications Production Department (SPDP), Council of Europe

Council of Europe Publishing
F-67075 Strasbourg Cedex
http://book.coe.int

ISBN 978-92-871-6694-4
© Council of Europe, December 2009
Printed at the Council of Europe

Pompidou Group

The Co-operation Group to Combat Drug Abuse and Illicit Trafficking in Drugs (Pompidou Group) is an intergovernmental body formed in 1971. Since 1980 it has carried out its activities within the framework of the Council of Europe, and 35 countries are now members of this European forum, which allows policy makers, professionals and experts to exchange information and ideas on a whole range of drug misuse and trafficking problems. Its mission is to contribute to the development of multidisciplinary, innovative, effective and evidence-based drug policies in its member states. It seeks to link policy, practice and science.

By setting up its Group of Experts in Epidemiology of Drug Problems in 1982, the Pompidou Group was a precursor of the development of drug research and monitoring of drug problems in Europe. The multi-city study, which aimed to assess, interpret and compare drug-use trends in Europe, is one of its major achievements. Other significant contributions include the piloting of a range of indicators (treatment-demand indicator) and methodological approaches, such as a methodology for school surveys which gave rise to the ESPAD (European School Survey Project on Alcohol and other Drugs).[1]

The Research Platform has superseded the group of experts in epidemiology active between 1982 and 2004. There has been a change of function, from developing data collection and monitoring methodologies to assessing the impact of research on policy. This started with the Strategic Conference on Linking Research, Policy and Practice – Lessons Learned, Challenges Ahead, which identified as a major gap the lack of exchange of knowledge.

The Research Platform's prime role is to support better the use of research evidence in policy and practice, thus promoting evidence-based policy. It also draws attention to the latest issues arising from drug research in the social and biomedical fields and promotes interaction between research disciplines such as these and psychological drug research. Reports on these subjects have been published regularly. One of the latest achievements is the online register on current drug research projects, set up in 2007 in collaboration with the EMCDDA (European Monitoring Centre for Drugs and Drug Addiction) to improve the lack of exchange of knowledge.

The Pompidou Group has a mandate to signal the latest findings from policy, science and practice. The Research Platform has the task to identify the latest findings in social drug research, psychological drug research and drug research in the biomedical field.

---

1. See the list of Pompidou Group documents and publications at the end of this publication.

This publication is hence an attempt to provide the latest signals from the three fields in addition to the latest findings from what is on offer and what may be offer in the area of treatment of drug addiction.

Contents

Summary

Chapter 1 – Cannabis in Europe: social research studies on dynamics in perception, policy and markets

Chapter 2 – Drug research: recent signals from the psychological field

Chapter 3 – Drug research: recent signals from the biomedical field

Chapter 4 – Initial assessment of the European Scientific Conference on "How can we better treat drug addiction? New scientific and clinical challenges for Europe"

Summary

As part and parcel of the functions of the Council of Europe's Pompidou Group, there is a mandate to signal the latest findings from policy, science and practice. Consequently, the Research Platform has sponsored three publications over the first part of the Work Programme 2007-10 that testify to the latest findings in social drug research, psychological drug research and drug research in the biomedical field. Moreover, it was deemed necessary to provide a further update for the second period, namely 2008-10. This publication is hence an attempt to provide the latest signals from the three fields in addition to the latest findings from what is on offer and what may be on offer in the treatment of drug addiction.

Social drug research

From the perspective of social drug research, the latest research findings are gleaned from the European Society for Social Drug Research (ESSD), which holds annual conferences on specific topics related to current concerns. The first publication to appear with the support of the Pompidou Group, *Research on drugs and drug policy from a European perspective*, contained selected peer-reviewed papers focusing on research on drugs and drug policy from a European standpoint. The second publication, *Cannabis in Europe: dynamics in perception, markets and policy*, was also the result of a ESSD annual conference on the same topic. In this publication, Professor Dirk Korf, Chairperson of the ESSD, provides us with a synthesis of both the conference and the subject matter itself.

Cannabis it would appear continues to be the most popular, by far, of all the illicit drugs in terms of use. In addition, it also seems to have had a renaissance among the middle-aged cohort as well as senior citizens. Thus, the focus on cannabis in the world of social drug research appears timely, and Professor Korf provides us with an overview of the salient points in this field. In turn, the synthesis is divided into eight sections, kicking off with an introduction on the use of cannabis through the 19th and 20th centuries and its eventual use as a psychoactive substance for pleasure in the 1960s. An interesting phenomena that is tackled in the second section is that of the link between cannabis use and schizophrenia. The point made here is that the increase in the use of cannabis did not give rise to a concomitant increase in the diagnosis of schizophrenia. Thus, it may be that it is a risk factor in a limited cohort, notably in those predisposed to the development of psychosis.

Section three deals with the topical issue of the use of cannabis in the young age cohort, highlighting the fact that age of first use really does depend on the age range in question. It would appear from what follows that cannabis use starts in late adolescence and that its prevalence seems to be unrelated to the type of policy in place in the respective country, be it liberal as in the Netherlands or repressive as in the case of Sweden. As regards policy, section five highlights the fact that there seems to be a shift from a more liberal perspective to one that is more repressive both in the Netherlands and Denmark. In relation to prevention which is specifically targeted at the young, universal prevention seems to miss the groups it is supposed to reach and thus selective prevention is suggested and that this is interactive and takes into account the needs of the cohort it is meant to be addressing (see section eight).

Section four covers the issue of cannabis dependence and suggests that the increase in the availability of services on offer has resulted in a significant number of people seeking treatment who would otherwise not have done so before, as nothing or very little was available. Thus, the increase in numbers does not signify an increase in cannabis-related problems. However, others would not agree, arguing that the increase is a result of the increased potency of cannabis grown in Europe. Overall, cannabis potency is akin to that otherwise imported and also the range of potency varies wildly. Most importantly and the crux of the issue is the fact that most users are able to regulate their intake of the drug and thus are able to compensate for increased or for that matter decreased potency.

Sections six and seven discuss the current trends in cannabis cultivation and the retail markets. With the increasing availability of technology and Internet sites that provide the necessary know how on growing your own cannabis, cultivation of cannabis in Europe has increased in a number of countries, which may in part be explained by users adopting the concept of "organic farming" or going green. Probably, and more importantly, self-provision removes the ghastly process through which one has to seek a dealer and risk the consequences of such acquaintances, which normally have criminal and other undesirable overtones. This latter point has major implications for the cannabis retail market in that in most instances people obtain their cannabis from their social network, out of the public eye and hence street dealing is now on the decline.

The last section, that is section nine, highlights the issue of the spread of cannabis availability and use after the political changes in Europe and the accession of most central and eastern European countries to the EU.

Psychological drug research

An update on the current signals from psychological drug research follows in the second chapter provided by Professor Jorge Negreiros, who also authored the first publication on this issue in 2006. Two main topics are tackled in the

overview provided, namely that of personality traits, and drug- and alcohol-related expectancies.

It is suggested that personality traits are usually defined as non-pathological factors related to thought patterns and behaviours involved in drug use. The psychological construct developed to date is that of behavioural disinhibition within which impulsivity and sensation seeking seem to be the traits mainly associated with alcohol and drug use.

Impulsivity has been defined in a number of ways but the key would appear to be the taking of decisions in an unplanned way with little regard to the negative outcome. It has also been suggested that impulsivity is part of a spectrum of disorders that fall under impulse control disorders and drug addiction per se may fall under this category (see below, Muscat). Moreover, it has been posited that impulsivity is multifaceted and thus it is imperative to underline which aspects are clearly related to the personality trait in question.

With these reservations in mind, a significant amount of work has gone into developing a model of impulsivity, namely the UPPS model, to try to understand impulsivity and its relation to substance abuse. The four dimensions of the model that are said to make up this construct of impulsivity are: urgency, lack of premeditation, lack of perseverance and sensation seeking. Of all these dimensions, urgency, to act rapidly without planning irrespective of a negative outcome, would seem to be the best predictor of alcohol and drug use. Moreover, from a cognitive perspective, reflection impulsivity appears to be a characteristic of substance dependence irrespective of the drug in question and continues to be present even after long periods of withdrawal from the drug.

Sensation seeking is a personality trait that implores one to find novel ways of gaining pleasurable experiences that also may be said to be of high stimulus impact. As an extreme example in the choice of sport such individuals would select, it would be more likely that they would opt for paragliding as opposed to table tennis. Sensation seeking also appears to have a biological basis as it is conjectured that the dopamine system involved in reward is somehow blunted and thus to obtain the same signal as others the stimulus needs to be of high impact, but that is not to say that environmental factors do not play a role. It is of interest, as pointed out by Negreiros, that sensation seeking is usually associated with increased frequency of drinking and the quantities consumed.

As far as modelling sensation seeking in the laboratory to get to grips with the underlying circuitry that substantiates such behaviour, Negreiros points us in the direction of the latest model which posits a role for serotonin (5-HT); more importantly the 5-HT7 receptor subtype is thought to be involved in the mediation of "attention and memory processes relevant to novelty induced arousal". In addition to serotonin, it is suggested that the peptide cholecystokinin (CCK) has a role in that it is normally associated with an anxiogenic response and this indeed has been found in animals exposed to alcohol or cocaine earlier on who produce this type of response when confronted by novelty later on. Two aspects are worthy of note at this point, namely that early exposure, or adolescent exposure, to alcohol or drugs increases responses to novelty, and, in the overview by Muscat in this edition, anxiety is the most notable psychiatric disorder that predates substance abuse.

The issue of drug and alcohol expectancies is not a new one and is related to the beliefs of the individual on the effects of these – both positive and negative, though mostly positive desirable experiences with the use of such substances. Thus these expectations have a major influence on the frequency and quantity of substance use. Two examples are given of studies conducted, in which, firstly, positive expectancies outweigh negative ones and thus frequency of use is related to such expectancy, whereas in a cohort of marijuana users, those using larger amounts were more likely to curtail use as result of negative expectancies.

To conclude, Negreiros cites the findings that impulsivity is better related to problem alcohol use whereas sensation seeking only alcohol use. Finally, he also cites the fact that at last an attempt has been made to integrate both personality traits and expectancies within the same model as opposed to these appearing as competing axioms in predicting substance abuse.

Biomedical drug research

The third chapter in this publication provides us with an update of the current theories in neuroscience that underpin our understanding of the neurobiological substrates involved in drug addiction. It begins with the latest findings in the clinical literature as these should provide the means through which one may better model substance dependence in the laboratory. There appear to be 10 characteristic clinical features that present in those diagnosed with substance dependence. Of these, the fact that the disorder occurs early in adulthood is indicative of the fact that use started earlier on and tolerance, withdrawal and relapse are the order of the day. Moreover, it is made explicit that psychiatric disorders are inextricably linked with substance abuse, and it is the psychiatric disorder that occurs first and not the other way round. Consequently, substance abuse does not arise as a result of lifestyle but may be attributed, most likely, to the presence of anxiety and, to a lesser extent, depression, which have clear neurobiological underpinnings within the brain.

Clearly, the main part of the text is dedicated to the three main stream theories of drug addiction currently holding pride of place. All it would appear concern the brain circuitry involved in acquiring reward, but it would appear that the emphasis of each of these three seems to shift between the different aspects of the same circuitry and the psychological constructs afforded to such. In the first one put forward by the Cambridge group, headed by Everitt and Robbins, which states that initiation of drug use activates the main structure, that is the ventral striatum, involved in reward, but maintenance is then taken over by an adjacent structure, the dorsal striatum, involved in response selection and it is this switch that gives rise to drug addiction. They also make the point on the basis of their laboratory model that impulsivity increases the likelihood of addiction and relapse. In short, this circuit is responsible for habit formation – in this case the formation of a bad habit.

Robinson and Berridge again cite the ventral striatum as the prime suspect but argue that it is the conditioning of cues related to drug use that is the driving motivation and not the reward per se, which becomes sensitised with repeated intake. In effect, from their perspective, drug addiction may be viewed as a condition in which the bias for drug-related stimuli has been amplified and which "gives impulsive drug longing a life of its own".

On the contrary, Koob and Le Moal view drug addiction as a problem of reward tolerance and suggest an alternative model in which drug addiction results as a consequence of the dysregulation of the homeostatic system of brain reward. In short, repetitive drug use results in a change in the reward set point, such that one needs to take on board more of the drug to get the same euphoric effects. This cycle of events leads to the body invoking what is termed as the allostatic response, which is only normally brought into play when the normal homeostatic mechanisms cannot cope and thus return the reward set point to its initial value. This allostatic response now becomes the modus operandi and is considered the basis for compulsive drug taking.

With respect to the brain mechanisms substantiating drug addiction, Tassin argues that in the case of the incentive sensitisation model posited by Robinson and Berridge, it is not the dopamine signal per se that has been compromised but the upstream circuits that feed into the reward pathway involved in maintaining attention to salient incoming stimuli. These in turn involve both noradrenaline and serotonin, and it is the uncoupling of this interaction which results in noradrenaline running free, which may account for the increased attention to drug stimuli as suggested by Robinson and Berridge above.

Relapse is also brought to the fore in that the laboratory models, such as the reinstatement model of relapse, have shown that conditioned cues, stress of one form or another and priming doses of the drug of abuse all reinstate responding or cause relapse. In addition, distal cues have also been considered using the same model and they would appear via the hippocampus and its input to the ventral striatum to provide information on context. This in itself has major implications with regard to treatment of drug addiction that aims at abstinence in different surroundings to that of drug use. In other words, abstinence should possibly be conducted in a number of contexts or environments including those associated with drug use.

The genetics of drug abuse provide the last instalment of this chapter as it is now understood that genetic heritability is of the order of some 50 % independent of the drug in question, and as high as 70 % for specific substances such as heroin. Substance dependence is also considered to be polygenic in the main; in that a number of genes acting in concert confer vulnerability to drug dependence but no single gene as such affords such a liability. As predicted in the previous publication on this issue, the way forward in tackling this issue, namely genome-wide association studies as opposed to single-gene candidate studies, was the development of a new technology, namely micro-arrays, in which the whole genome may be scanned. The use of such a technology has resulted in a number of genes coming to the fore that may be associated with drug addiction and include those that are involved in forming neuronal connections, enzymatic activity as well as ion channels and transport processes. All are expressed in the brain but the real breakthrough here is the finding that genes involved in forming nerve cell connections in development and expressed in brain areas such as the hippocampus – important in laying the foundations for memory – may in turn explain why the propensity for relapse in recovered addicts persists for many years. Finally, the section concludes with a suggestion of late that dependence per se may resemble impulse control disorders and from a genetic standpoint in family and twin studies on impulsivity they account for up to 60 % of the variance for the risk of dependency/addiction. Moreover, a reduction in the availability of the dopamine D2 receptors in human and animal studies provides a basis for a possible mechanism for both impulsivity and the development of addiction/dependence.

Drug treatment

The final chapter in this update includes an overview by Dominique Vuillaume of the conference held by the French presidency in December 2008 that addressed the topical issue of drug treatment and was entitled "How can we better treat drug addiction? New scientific and clinical challenges for Europe". In effect, what can research tell us about the mechanisms that give rise to drug addiction in order that we may be able to better design drug treatment, prevention and integration strategies. With regard to lifetime prevalence, some 70 million Europeans have tried cannabis at least once, this then falls to 12 million for second placed cocaine, followed closely by amphetamines, some 11 million, and then by ecstasy, 9.5 million, while it is reported there are some 2.1 million problem opiate-dependent drug users in Europe. In light of these figures, the challenges for Europe it is argued are related to public health in the main together with the social consequences that arise with such use. Above all, the need to understand human behaviour is paramount if one is to understand addiction and this requires research to be conducted in an interdisciplinary fashion if it is to address the situation holistically and not in a piecemeal way.

The overview is divided into seven sections that relate to the thematic sessions of the conference. Neurobiological advances in our understanding of drug addiction opens the thematic sessions and draws on Tassin's work on the decoupling of the upstream interaction between noradrenaline and serotonin as the basis for a dysfunctional dopamine system in addiction. Details of Piazza's work follow, according to which, as in human subjects, only some 15-17% of animals go on to become addicted when given access to drugs of abuse and this as a result of the two phenotypes associated with the disorder: namely, high reactivity to stress, anxiety and impulsivity and another, which may be the main one, related to compulsive drug taking and loss of control, of which little is known. Finally, the European project IMAGEN was introduced, which will attempt to combine genetic studies and neuroimaging on a cohort of some 2 000 14 year-olds to assess risk phenotypes for mental disorders and/or drug addiction on the basis of clinical, behavioural, cognitive and imaging data.

New approaches for treating cocaine addiction are then examined, with the main focus on the new cocaine vaccine invented by Professor Kosten. It has been found to be effective in 70-75% of those who responded. In contrast, the final part of this session was dedicated to psychosocial treatments for cocaine, which may be narrowed down to three: namely, cognitive behavioural therapy, contingency management and strengthening social ties, where contingency management seems to be leading the way in terms of encouraging results and more widespread use.

Community-based approaches have had a good look at therapeutic communities (TCs) over the past 40 years or so, and the most important factor that seems to emerge is duration of care and assistance. However, TCs add no more value than other forms of residential treatment.

Like TCs, opiate substitution has been in place in the United States for some 40 years and to a lesser degree in countries across Europe. However, the positive impact of both methadone and buprenorphine is clear for all to see as far as the reduction in the use of illegal drugs, injecting use, syringe sharing and criminal behaviour.

The highlight of the fifth session relates to the current treatment options for young problematic users of cannabis. Once again, the United States seems to lead the way in that in 2000 family-based treatment was established and this is now the focus of a European effort involving five countries to assess the clinical effectiveness of this type of new intervention. To date, of the patients assessed in France and Germany, family-based intervention proved to be superior to the current treatments on offer in that there was a greater reduction in consumption of cannabis among this cohort of dependent users.

"Change without treatment" was the title given to the penultimate session, which covered the area of self-change without resorting to traditional intervention methods. It is becoming clear that those who are able to regulate or stop their use of drugs have a less intense dependency profile and no psychiatric co-morbidity, as compared to those who opt for treatment.

Finally, the last session was devoted to a debate on how one may better organise research centred on drug treatment at the European level. It was acknowledged that research in this area is fragmented and sources of funding are inconsistent and depend on the individual areas of study. Some efforts at getting to grips with who is doing what in Europe in the area of drug research have been made with the launch of the online register of current drug research by the Pompidou Group. More needs to be done, but it is vital that basic research in the field of addiction neurosciences needs to be preserved.

Chapter 1 – Cannabis in Europe: social research studies on dynamics in perception, policy and markets[2]

by Professor Dirk J. Korf, Director of the Bonger Institute of Criminology at the University of Amsterdam and Chairperson of the ESSD

1. Introduction: focus on cannabis

Cannabis has been used in Europe for centuries, both for treating physical ailments and for the psychoactive qualities of the drug. In the late 19th and early 20th centuries, hashish played a significant role as a medicine, but that was quickly to change (Fankhauser, 2008). After a timid re-entry as a psychoactive substance in the 1950s and early 1960s, the spread of cannabis use accelerated, and from the late 1960s it became an increasingly collective phenomenon.

Drugs have social meanings, both for users and for non-users. Not only can the same substance (say, cannabis) have different meanings at the same time, but the social meaning of a particular drug can also change drastically over time (Fountain and Korf, 2007). Whereas initially, in the 1960s and early 1970s, the modern use of hashish and marijuana was strongly associated with deviancy and mental health problems, as well as with countercultures, the realisation slowly dawned that the vast majority of cannabis users were people who held jobs or attended school or college. Far from being under the spell of cannabis, they just used it for personal recreation. Cannabis came to be less and less an element of deviant lifestyles; the former dividing line between users and non-users began to blur. This development led Parker, Aldridge and Measham (1998) to speak of normalisation.

Today, some four decades after the revival of cannabis use in Europe, old paradigms are having renewed appeal. While social scientists were convinced that the pathologisation of cannabis use would gradually fade, they are now forced to recognise, sometimes to their undisguised disappointment (Schneider, 2008), that no such development has occurred. Powerful advances in biomedical and neuropsychological research have delivered more and more information about the genetic aspects of drug use and addiction and about the actions of drugs on the brain. Drug addiction is often referred to nowadays as a brain disease.

---

2. This paper is an extended version of the introductory and summarising chapter of the European Society for Social Drug Research (ESSD) book on cannabis.

Yet drugs are more than just chemical substances that influence individual human behaviour through their effects on the brain. As Zinberg (1984) showed, a drug user's personality, attitudes, expectancies and motivations – and particularly the settings in which drug use occurs – have a greater influence on both the user and his or her drug-taking patterns than a drug's pharmacological properties. These are issues that lie squarely in the realms of sociology, anthropology, psychology and criminology.

2. Cannabis and schizophrenia

The past few years have seen a profusion of writings on the subject of cannabis and schizophrenia. Indeed, the insights into this phenomenon are now far more precise than they once were. Yet it seems as if a new generation of researchers is poorly acquainted with the older literature on the subject, thus leaving the impression that the relation between cannabis use and schizophrenia is a new discovery. Perhaps that is because the phenomenon now called "cannabis schizophrenia" was formerly referred to as "cannabis psychosis" – a term that still exists today but now refers solely to certain acute effects of cannabis use. Undoubtedly, this hiatus in historical awareness can be blamed on the fact that many older publications are not available on the Internet – the quintessential literature search medium for the researchers of today.

Whilst the evidence for cannabis use as a causal factor in psychosis seems to steadily mount, the French researcher Vuillaume (Chapter 4) points out that many open questions still exist. Most of these lie in the field of the natural sciences, but a no less important socio-epidemiologic issue is that the increase in cannabis use has not automatically been accompanied by a meaningful rise in the number of young people diagnosed with psychosis in clinical settings.

3. Cannabis and youth

Another factor that figures heavily in the altered discourse on cannabis is the adolescent use of the drug and the risk of cannabis dependence. School surveys are a relatively simple and cost-attractive instrument to map drug-use prevalence amongst adolescents. Thanks partly to vigorous support from the Pompidou Group of the Council of Europe, surveys of secondary school pupils aged 15 and 16 have been held regularly for years in many European countries. This European School Survey Project on Alcohol and Other Drugs (ESPAD) has produced a wealth of information about trends and patterns in adolescent substance use. Cannabis comfortably scores the highest of all illicit drugs (Hibell et al., 2004). At the same time, wide divergences in cannabis use exist within Europe. In some countries, almost half of the surveyed adolescents report having smoked cannabis at some time, against only tiny percentages in other countries. At first sight, it would seem that lifetime prevalence may be linked to national cannabis policies. The Dutch figures, for example, are several times higher than the Swedish ones, which could lead one to conclude that a repressive approach – of which Sweden is traditionally the benchmark – discourages cannabis use more effectively than policies like the Dutch ones, which are seen as tolerant. But why, then, are the prevalence rates in countries like the Czech Republic, France, Ireland and the UK higher than those in the Netherlands? And why do adolescents in nations with greatly differing cannabis policies, such as Belgium, Germany, Italy, Slovakia and Slovenia, have approximately the same prevalence rates as the Netherlands?

School surveys harbour the risk of making drug use seem chiefly an adolescent phenomenon. In reality, many people who try cannabis do not do so until after age 16, and are therefore too old to be spotted by the ESPAD survey. "Age of first use" depends on the age-group surveyed. The wider the age range in a survey, the higher the age of first use. In the Dutch general population survey of 2005, for example, the average age of first cannabis use in the 15-24 age-group was 16.4 years, but for the wider 15-64 age category it was 19.6 years (Rodenburg et al., 2007). In the German household study of 2006, the lifetime prevalence of cannabis use was higher in the 21-29 age-group than in the 18-20 category, at 42 % versus 34 % (Kraus et al., 2008). Yet even though cannabis use is not a typical youth phenomenon, the current use of the drug does tend to be highest in late adolescence and early adulthood. The German survey, for one, reported peak use in the 18-20 age-group (18 % last-year prevalence, 9 % last-month prevalence) and the 21-24 age-group (17 % and 7 % respectively); at the same time, some people in their 30s, 40s, 50s and 60s were found to be smoking cannabis as well. The study thus confirms a European trend towards increasing current use of cannabis by middle-aged people and senior citizens (EMCDDA, 2008).

4. Cannabis dependence and marijuana potency

In recent years, many European countries have reported significant increases in the numbers of clients presenting to addiction services with cannabis problems. They are of notably younger age than clients with hard drug problems (Montanari, Taylor and Griffiths, 2008). The German survey cited above confirms that adolescents and young adults aged 18-24 are more likely (with rates of 3-4 %) than people above that age to qualify for a DSM-IV diagnosis of cannabis dependence. The lower figure for the 25-29 age-group (1 %), and the still lower percentages for older groups, suggest that cannabis dependence may for many people be a temporary condition characterised by natural recovery. The German researchers also concluded that the 12-month prevalence of cannabis dependence remained stable from 1997 to 2006. Possibly, then, the growing numbers of cannabis clients in the European addiction services can be more readily attributed to changing ideas about cannabis use – and to concomitant shifts in referral practices and a widened availability of services – than to any real increase in cannabis-related problems. Although

Simon and Kraus (2008: 306) have established for Germany that a quintupling of demand for cannabis treatment in the period 1992-2003 "reflects a genuine increase in clinically diagnosable cases of cannabis use disorders", Montanari, Taylor and Griffiths (2008: 275) conclude for Europe as a whole that "a substantial proportion of those referred [for treatment] appear not to be intensive cannabis users".

An oft-heard explanation for the growing numbers of cannabis clients is the sharply increased potency of marijuana (King, 2008). All over Europe in recent years, market substitution has occurred, with herbal cannabis, or marijuana, increasingly supplanting resin cannabis, or hashish (UNODC, 2007). The bulk of this marijuana is grown in Europe, and it is indeed higher in THC than its counterparts imported from other regions (King, Griffiths and Carpentier, 2004). That is because most domestic European marijuana is cultivated indoors, using innovations ranging from high-yield seeds to novel grow techniques. At the same time, wide variations in marijuana potency exist both within and between countries (King, 2008); in the Netherlands – the country where trends in THC content are monitored the most systematically – the potency of European marijuana has been found comparable to that of imported hashish (Niesink et al., 2008). It follows that market substitution does not necessarily run parallel to a rising consumption of higher-potency cannabis. Moreover, users of cannabis with a higher THC content are able to moderate their intake, using self-regulatory techniques like putting less cannabis into a joint or inhaling the smoke less deeply (Korf, Benschop and Wouters, 2007).

5. Changing cannabis policies

Denmark and the Netherlands are the European countries with long-standing reputations for "liberal" cannabis policies. In both countries, a noticeable swing has occurred towards increasing repression in recent years. In Copenhagen, the numerous marijuana stalls in the park in Christiania have been shut down by police, and the policy of tolerating "hash clubs" was also brought to an end (Asmussen, 2007). A new Danish response to cannabis has been to introduce treatment for cannabis problems among prison inmates. Dahl, Asmussen Frank and Kolind (2008) explore the interrelationship between drug control and cannabis treatment in Danish prisons, and they discuss how changes in national drug legislation and cannabis policy have influenced the development of cannabis treatment as well as its outcomes.

Although the sale of cannabis is still allowed in the Dutch "cannabis coffee shops", policy shifts in recent years have had a drastic impact on the stocking of these officially tolerated selling points. Wouters (2008) recounts how thousands of marijuana cultivation sites in the Netherlands are currently being raided and dismantled and large numbers of marijuana plants confiscated and destroyed.

An interesting highlight of the Danish and Dutch contributions is their analysis of how changes in government cannabis policy are shaped on the ground, and in particular how the original plans and aims of higher-echelon policy makers become concretely implemented by lower-echelon "street-level bureaucrats" (Lipsky, 1980) – along with the unforeseen risks and unintended effects that can arise in the process.

6. Domestic cannabis cultivation

The vast quantities of marijuana seized in the Netherlands each year stand in stark contrast to the small numbers of plants cultivated by most of the home growers interviewed by the Belgian criminologist Decorte (2008). A remarkable number of them make no use of modern growing techniques for indoor cultivation, but grow their plants outdoors on a very small scale. Besides the financial advantages of growing their own marijuana, a prime motive lies in the pleasure they derive from seeing their own plants grow. Normative considerations, such as avoiding contacts with criminal dealers in the commercial cannabis market, may also play a role. Building on the thesis that cannabis markets have the least damaging consequences when they are the least populated by criminal enterprisers, Decorte initiates an appeal for what one might call harm reduction on the supply side of the cannabis market. Government-tolerated "hobby cultivation" could help destabilise the role of criminal organisations.

According to opponents of the 2004 liberalisation of UK cannabis legislation, developments have been triggered that already justify reversing this decision. One of their arguments is that downgrading cannabis to a Class C (least harmful) drug has fostered an increase in domestic production – thereby inducing more cannabis use. Drawing partly on his own fieldwork as well as on interviews with different types of marijuana growers and a range of professionals, the criminologist Potter (2008) subjects this claim to critical scrutiny and offers alternative explanations for the spread of domestic cannabis cultivation.

7. Cannabis retail markets

At the consumer level, the cannabis market is characterised by small-scale activities, so concludes the German researcher Werse (2008) on the basis of his research in Frankfurt-on-Main. Using a fine combination of quantitative and qualitative data, he describes and analyses the characteristics of an urban retail cannabis market. Many cannabis users do not buy their own hashish or marijuana, but satisfy their needs by sharing joints. Many consumer-level cannabis transactions also conceal themselves from the public eye in that the drug is sold mainly within informal social networks of friends and acquaintances – who are expressly not labelled as dealers. The phenomenon is sustained by cannabis prohibition, and it enables frequent users to earn enough for their personal smoking needs by selling to others. Only a small market segment is left to street dealers, who are mostly "outsiders" – usually migrants who have much less social access to the informal peer networks of "established" cannabis users. For the street dealers, selling cannabis and other drugs is basically a survival strategy, although it also commands respect and boosts their status within their own circles (Bucerius, 2007).

Research by Stevenson (2008) in Northern Ireland concurs with Werse's findings in many ways, but interesting contrasts also emerge. As in Germany, informal peer networks play a significant role in the supply of cannabis to consumers. Northern Irish cannabis users also prefer not to call their suppliers "dealers", but "friends who deal" or simply "sellers". But whilst Werse concentrates on the retail level, Stevenson's essay also highlights middle- and upper-level suppliers – and in the eyes of cannabis users and small-scale suppliers, it is mainly (but not only) these suppliers who are the "real dealers". Stevenson persuasively elucidates how social control and respectability among cannabis users relates to the type of cannabis supplier they patronise. Fearing intimidation by criminals, arrest by police or discovery by employers, cannabis users with sensitive jobs avoid any contact with "real dealers" and rely entirely on trusted friends. This contrasts with users from lower socio-economic classes or holding non-professional jobs, who see no point in concealing their cannabis use from employers and are comfortable contacting anyone to obtain cannabis.

8. Drug prevention for vulnerable young people

Under drug policy, law enforcement primarily targets the supply side of the market. The demand side is typically the work domain of prevention and treatment services. Prevention has many forms, ranging from drug and alcohol education for adolescents who have never taken any drugs to harm reduction efforts targeting groups of experienced users. Schools undertake substance use prevention activities everywhere in Europe, albeit with wide variations in methods and intensity. Some characteristics in common are information provision (which may or may not be combined with other components like social skills training), mainly classroom delivery, and a primary focus on pupils in early adolescence (roughly aged 12 to 15). When it comes to illicit substances, the chief emphasis is logically on cannabis, since that is normally the first drug that young people come into contact with, and the one with the highest prevalence of use by far.

An advantage of prevention activities like these is they are capable of reaching large groups in a relatively simple, cost-effective manner. A major drawback is that the very groups with the highest risks of taking drugs and developing drug-related problems are less effectively reached, or not at all. This typically involves truants and school dropouts, but other examples are adolescents in residential treatment for emotional or conduct disorders. The latter group is the focus of research by Vander Laenen and De Wree (2008).

Of particular interest in their study is their innovative methodological approach, which they combine with authentic curiosity about the role that cannabis plays in the life worlds and mindsets of these young people. They also report the views these adolescents express as to the dos and don'ts of drug prevention.

9. Vocal cannabis users

By and large, the spread of cannabis took place earlier and on a larger scale in the countries of western Europe than in those of central and eastern Europe. Political changes – in particular the removal of the Iron Curtain, the subsequent relaxation of border controls, and the free movement of people and goods between more and more new EU member states – brought with it an upsurge in the availability and use of cannabis. Notwithstanding this, striking differences still exist between the countries in question in terms of the pace and scale of the spread of cannabis (Moskalewicz et al., 2008). Hungary is one central European country where the number of cannabis users has grown rather rapidly. Sárosi and Demetrovics (2008) describe and analyse the diverse reactions in the Hungarian political arena and public debate to the emergence of cannabis use. Following a period of increasingly stringent legislation, a policy shift occurred, and it also created more latitude for civil movements campaigning for legalisation or decriminalisation of cannabis. An interesting aspect is how movements such as these, like organisations of professionals, reach across borders and increasingly work together with movements in other European countries.

References

Asmussen, V. (2007), "Danish cannabis policy in practice: The closing of 'Pusher Street' and the cannabis market in Copenhagen", in Fountain J. and Korf, D.J. (eds), *Drugs in society. European perspectives.* Oxford: Radcliffe, 14-27.

Bucerius, S.M. (2007), "'What else should I do?' Cultural influences on the drug trade of migrants in Germany", *Journal of Drug Issues*, 37 (3), 673-697.

Dahl, H.V., Asmussen Frank, V. and Kolind, T. (2008), "Cannabis treatment in Danish prisons: a product of new directions in national drug policy?", in Korf, D.J. (ed.), *Cannabis in Europe: dynamics in perception, policy and markets,* Lengerich, Germany: Pabst Science Publishers.

Decorte, T. (2008), "Domestic marijuana cultivation in Belgium: on (un) intended effects of drug policy on the cannabis market", in Korf, D.J. (ed.), *Cannabis in Europe: dynamics in perception, policy and markets*, Lengerich, Germany: Pabst Science Publishers.

EMCDDA (2007), *State of the drugs problem in Europe. Annual report 2007*, Lisbon: EMCDDA.

EMCDDA (2008), "Substance use among older adults: a neglected problem", *Drugs in Focus*, April 2008, Lisbon: EMCDDA.

Fankhauser, M. (2008), "Cannabis as medicine in Europe in the 19th century", in Rödner Sznitman, S., Olsson, B. and Room, R. (eds), *A cannabis reader: global issues and local experiences*, Lisbon: EMCDDA Monographs, 8 (Volume I), 3-14.

Fountain, J. and Korf, D.J. (eds) (2007), *Drugs in society. European perspectives*, Oxford: Radcliffe.

Hibell, B., Andersson, B., Bjarnason, T., Ahlström, S., Balakivera, O., Kokkevi, A. and Morgan, M. (2004), *The ESPAD report 2003. Alcohol and other drug use among students in 35 European countries*, Stockholm: CAN.

King, L.A. (2008), "Understanding cannabis potency and monitoring cannabis products in Europe", in Rödner Sznitman, S., Olsson, B. and Room, R. (eds), *A cannabis reader: global issues and local experiences*, Lisbon: EMCDDA Monographs, 8 (Volume I), 239-259.

King, L.A., Griffiths, P. and Carpentier, C. (2004), *An overview of cannabis potency in Europe*, Lisbon: EMCDDA.

Korf, D.J., Benschop, A. and Wouters, M. (2007), "Differential responses to cannabis potency: a typology of users based on self-reported consumption behaviour", *The International Journal of Drug Policy*, 18, 168-176.

Kraus, L., Pfeiffer-Gerschel, T. and Pabst, A. (2008), "Cannabis und andere illegale Drogen: Prävalenz, Konsummuster und Trends", *Ergebnisse des epidemiologischen Suchtsurveys 2006. Sucht*, 45 (Supplement 1), 16-25.

Lipsky, M. (1980), *Street-level bureaucracy. Dilemmas of the individual in public services*. New York: The Russel Sage Foundation.

Montanari, L., Taylor, C. and Griffiths, P. (2008), "Cannabis users in treatment in Europe: an analysis from treatment demand data", in Rödner Sznitman, S., Olsson, B. and Room, R. (cds), *A cannabis reader: global issues and local experiences*, Lisbon: EMCDDA Monographs, 8 (Volume II), 261-276.

Moskalewicz, J., Alaste, A.A., Demetrovics, Z., Kelmova, D. and Sieroslawski, J. (2008), "Enlargement 2005: cannabis in the new EU member states", in Rödner Sznitman, S., Olsson, B. and Room, R. (eds), *A cannabis reader: global issues and local experiences*, Lisbon: EMCDDA Monographs, 8 (Volume I), 63-93.

Niesink, R., Rigter, S., Hoek, J. and Goldschmidt, H. (2008), *THC-concentraties in wiet, nederwiet en hasj in Nederlandse coffeeshops (2007-2008)*, Utrecht: Trimbos Institute.

Parker, H., Aldridge, J. and Measham, F. (1998), *Illegal leisure. The normalization of adolescent recreational drug use*, London: Routledge.

Potter, G. (2008), "The growth of cannabis cultivation: explanations for import substitution in the UK", in Korf, D.J. (ed.), *Cannabis in Europe: dynamics in perception, policy and markets*, Lengerich, Germany: Pabst Science Publishers.

Rodenburg, G., Spijkerman, R., van den Eijnden, R. and van den Mheen, D. (2007), *Nationaal Prevalentie Onderzoek Middelengebruik 2005*, Rotterdam: IVO.

Sárosi, P. and Demetrovics, Z. (2008), "Cannabis in Hungary: drug policy, legislation and civil movements", in Korf, D.J. (ed.), *Cannabis in Europe: dynamics in perception, policy and markets*, Lengerich, Germany: Pabst Science Publishers.

Schneider, W. (2008), "Cannabis: Gefahr für die Jugend? Kritische Anmerkungen zur aktuellen Cannabisdebatte", *Wiener Zeitschrift für Suchtforschung*, 29(1/2), 15-26.

Simon, R. and Kraus, L. (2008), "Has treatment demand for cannabis-related disorders increased in Germany?", in Rödner Sznitman, S., Olsson, B. and Room, R. (eds), *A cannabis reader: global issues and local experiences*, Lisbon: EMCDDA Monographs, 8 (Volume II), 305-323.

Stevenson, C. (2008), "Cannabis supply in Northern Ireland. Perspectives from users", in Korf, D.J. (ed.), *Cannabis in Europe: dynamics in perception, policy and markets*, Lengerich, Germany: Pabst Science Publishers.

UNODC (2007), *World drug report 2007*, Vienna: UNODC.

Vander Laenen, F. and De Wree, E. (2008), "Why the prevention of cannabis use does not work: vulnerable young people's analysis", in Korf, D.J. (ed.), *Cannabis in Europe: dynamics in perception, policy and markets*, Lengerich, Germany: Pabst Science Publishers.

Werse, B. (2008), "Retail markets for cannabis users, sharers, go-betweens and stash dealers", in Korf, D.J. (ed.), *Cannabis in Europe: dynamics in perception, policy and markets*, Lengerich, Germany: Pabst Science Publishers.

Wouters, M. (2008), "Controlling cannabis cultivation in the Netherlands", in Korf, D.J. (ed.), *Cannabis in Europe: dynamics in perception, policy and markets*, Lengerich, Germany: Pabst Science Publishers.

Zinberg, N.E. (1984), *Drug, set and setting: the basis for controlled intoxicant use*, New Haven: Yale University Press.

Chapter 2 – Drug research: recent signals from the psychological field

by Professor Jorge Negreiros, Faculty of Psychology and Education Sciences, University of Porto

1. Overview

The goal of this report is to collect signals from drug research undertaken recently in the psychological field. This exercise will take as a starting point the research findings in drug psychology described in a previous publication (Negreiros, 2006). Two major topics will be reviewed: personality traits; and alcohol- and drug-related expectancies. I will start with a short summary pointing out the major findings in each of these domains and then give an update of the results of recent research. The final section will focus on the strengths and limitations in both of these areas of psychological drug research.

2. Signals from psychological drug research

2.1. Personality traits

Personality traits are usually defined as non-pathological factors related to thought patterns and behaviours involved in drug use. The association of personality traits with tobacco use, abuse and dependence has been extensively documented during the past 20 years. (Associations have also been shown with regard to alcohol and illegal drugs.) Different personality traits have shown an association with drug abuse. Nevertheless, recent efforts seem to be based on the general construct of disinhibition or behavioural disinhibition (Watson and Clark, 1993; Conway et al., 2003; Magid, MacLean and Colder, 2007). Although several facets have been examined in relation to this personality construct, impulsivity and sensation seeking are among the most stable and strong personality traits of alcohol and drug involvement (Negreiros, 2006).

2.1.1. Impulsivity

Impulsivity is defined as an individual's tendency to make rapid behavioural changes regardless of negative consequences or the loss of a postponed reward of greater intensity (for example, taking a drug despite knowing the potential adverse effects on health). Impulsivity has also been described as a "consistent tendency for persons to show fast or slow decision times in situations of high uncertainty". Previous research has demonstrated an association between substance use and impulsivity. Several studies have shown that increased impulsivity is present across users of different drugs of abuse including alcohol, nicotine, cocaine and amphetamines (Cf. Negreiros, 2006).

Recent signals from research on impulsivity and drug use

Recent work on this personality trait and its relationship with drug abuse has been rather prolific (for example, Doran, McChargue and Spring, 2008; Oswald et al., 2007; Vassileva et al., 2007; Lejuez et al., 2007; Verdejo-Garcia et al., 2006a, 2006b, 2007; Clark et al., 2006; Billieux, Lindena and Ceschia, 2006; Ryb et al., 2006; Dom et al., 2006; Dafters, 2005).

As indicated before (Negreiros, 2006), a major limitation of research on impulsivity and drug abuse concerns the lack of agreement that still exists on how impulsivity should be defined and measured. Although impulsivity is considered a multifactorial construct it is not clear which dimensions are more appropriate to define this personality trait.

It is important to note that significant achievements have been made recently in this area. Several empirical studies have examined in further detail the relationship between separate dimensions of impulsivity and substance dependence. A large body of this research has been concentrated in the UPPS model (Whiteside and Lynam, 2001) for understanding impulsive behaviour (Magid and Colder, 2007; Verdejo-Garcia et al., 2007; Anestis, Selby and Joiner, 2007). The UPPS model maintains that there are four personality dimensions that are related differentially to impulsive behaviours: urgency, sensation seeking, lack of premeditation and lack of perseverance (Whiteside and Lynam, 2001).

Verdejo-Garcia et al. (2007) used the UPPS Impulsive Behaviour Scale to examine differences between 36 individuals with substance dependence and 36 drug-free controls on four dimensions of the scale. They found that urgency "was the best predictor of severity of medical, employment, alcohol, drug, family/social, legal and psychiatric problems" (p. 213) in the individuals with substance dependence. This same dimension of impulsivity (urgency) was also found to be associated with cigarette craving (Billieux, Lindena and Ceschia, 2006). In a similar way, Anestis, Selby and Joiner (2007), using the UPPS Impulsive Behaviour Scale, found that urgency, defined as the tendency, specially in the presence of a negative affect, to act rapidly and without plan- ning, was associated with three maladaptive behaviours: excessive reassurance seeking, drinking to cope and bulimic symptoms. In a recent study (Magid and Colder, 2007), the four factor structure of the Impulsive Behaviour Scale was confirmed, demonstrating the four sub-scales' "differential relations with alcohol use and problems" (p. 1927) in college students.

In association with this concern, some studies have examined the relationship of cognitive or motor impulsivity with the use of different types of drugs. Clark et al. (2006) have analysed the concept of "reflection impulsivity" – defined as the tendency to get together and evaluate information before making a decision – in current substance users, who were dependent on either amphetamines or opiates. The study demonstrated that current substance users, who were dependent on these psychoactive substances, gathered significantly less information than control subjects. The authors recognise that "reduced reflection is a stable cognitive characteristic in substance dependence, which occurs irrespective of the drug of abuse and persists with prolonged abstinence" (p. 520). In another study (Verdejo-Garcia, Perales and Pérez-Garcia, 2006a), cocaine and heroin abstinent polysubstance abusers showed impulsivity deficits in several measures of cognitive impulsivity when compared to controls. It is noteworthy that only cocaine abstinent polysubstance abusers showed deficits in measures of response inhibition; both heroin and cocaine abstinent polysubstance abusers showed significant deficits in decision making compared to controls. The results of a study conducted by Dafters (2005) also support the view that ecstasy users who also used cannabis are more impulsive than non-users. Nevertheless, the results did not support a connection between impulsivity and the specific inhibitory processes examined in the study. Finally, in a stable, abstinent alcohol-dependent population, it was found that "behavioural disinhibition and delay discounting are two independent dimensions of impulsivity and that decision-making is a third cognitive dimension, independent of both other measures" (Dom et al., 2006: 465).

2.1.2. Sensation seeking

Sensation seeking is a personality trait characterised by the extent of a person's desire for novelty and intensity of sensory stimulation and experiences (Andrew and Cronin, 1997). This personality trait is considered to be influenced by both biological (for example, low basal dopaminergic activity) and environmental factors. Sensation seeking has been indicated as a potent precursor of drug abuse as well as a personality feature that strongly influences drug-use patterns (Negreiros, 2006).

Recent signals from research on sensation seeking and drug use

Recent work on sensation seeking and substance use corroborates the results of previous studies supporting a relationship between this personality trait and the use of different psychoactive substances, thus extending and validating the association (Fisher and Smith, 2007; Legrand et al., 2007; Magid, MacLean and Colder, 2007; Alessio, Balocco and Laghi, 2006; Gurpegui et al., 2007).

The association between sensation seeking and alcohol use has generated the largest body of research in the past 20 years. This tendency also remains evident in more recent research. Higher levels of sensation seeking are in general correlated with greater quantity and frequency of alcohol use. A recent meta-analysis, which examined the association between sensation seeking and alcohol use (Hittner and Swickert, 2006), corroborates this general finding. The analysis, based on 61 studies, demonstrated a small to moderate-size effect between alcohol use and sensation seeking (rw = .263). Of the four sensation-seeking components, disinhibition showed the largest mean effect size (rw = .368). Disinhibition is often the strongest sensation-seeking dimension of alcohol use. This same result was also evident in a recent study conducted by Legrand and colleagues (2007), from the University of Reims Champagne Ardenne (France). In fact, the results supported the relationship between disinhibition and blood-alcohol concentration among women, measured at the end of an "open bar" party. In men, "experience seeking was found to be of equal significance as disinhibition" (p. 1950).

Recent research on sensation seeking has also made considerable advances in clarifying the underlying neuropharmacological mechanisms involved in novelty-seeking behaviours, especially in animals (Ballaz, Akil and Watson, 2007a, 2007b). Using rat models, these studies are based on the diversity of behavioural responses rats exhibit in an impossible-to-avoid novel environment, assuming that novelty-seeking behaviour in the rat is similar to some aspects of sensation seeking in humans. Basically, in those environments, some animals are highly active (high responders) while others show fewer tendencies for exploration and behave in a more anxious manner (low responders). Ballaz, Akil and Watson (2007a) demonstrated that response to novelty in rats might be associated to differential 5-HT mediated neurotransmission. More specifically, the 5-HT7 receptor "may mediate attentional and memory processes relevant to novelty-induced arousal" (Ballaz, Akil and Watson, 2007a). Moreover, brain cholecystokinin (CCK) and its receptor CCK (2), which has been implicated in the aetiology of anxiety, seem also to mediate adaptation to novelty-induced stress in rats. In another experiment using rat models (Stansfield and Kirstein, 2007), animals chronically exposed to cocaine or ethanol during adolescence showed a greater locomotor response in a novel environment and spend less time with a novel object. These behaviours "are indicative of a stress or anxiogenic response to novelty or a novel situation" (p. 637). One of the conclusions of the study is that chronic exposure to ethanol during adolescence increases responding to novelty "which subsequently may render the animal more likely to engage in continued drug use" (p. 641).

2.1.3. Drug expectancies

Drug expectancies have been defined as beliefs, both positive and negative, about the short term, or relatively immediate, effects of drugs on behaviour, mood and emotions. The decision to use alcohol or drugs is thought to be mediated by an individual's beliefs or expectancies about the desirable consequences of using drugs. Previous research has shown that one's expectations about the effects of using a specific type of drug are associated with the quantity and frequency of actual use. Extensive literature supports the importance of expectancies in predicting alcohol use, particularly in adolescents (Cf. Negreiros, 2006).

Recent signals from alcohol- and drug-related expectancies research

More recent work on drug-related expectancies research has extended the study of this association to the use of other substances. For example, Hayaki, Anderson and Stein (2007) examined the association between cocaine expectancies and frequency of use in a community sample of drug users. Results showed that frequency of cocaine use was positively associated with higher expectation that drug use would increase social and physical pleasure and inversely associated with higher expectation that drug use would increase cognitive and physical impairment. Lundahl and Lukas (2006) conducted an experiment on cocaine expectancies in a group of occasional non-dependent cocaine users involving an examination of expected cocaine effect and actual response to cocaine administration. Findings showed that only negative expectancies were related to subjective responses to actual cocaine use. In fact, global positive expectancies were associated with "two indices of positive subjective response"; global negative expectancies "were significantly correlated with subjective cocaine effects that are generally interpreted as positive effects" (p. 1269).

In the Department of Clinical Psychology at the University of Munich, Demmel, Nicolai and Gregorzik (2006) have examined the relationship between alcohol expectancies and current mood state in social drinkers. The findings indicated that affective state was related to the evaluation of alcohol's effects, suggesting the emotional state may influence drinking behaviour by changing the strength of alcohol-related cognitions.

Some recent studies have also examined associations between marijuana expectancies and different aspects related to the use of this psychoactive substance. In one of these studies (Simmons and Arens, 2007) expectancies of negative consequences were found significantly associated with marijuana-use intensity, with individuals who used higher quantities reporting that negative consequences were more likely. In another study (Gaher and Simons, 2007), the authors demonstrated that individuals choose not to use marijuana largely due to concerns about potential negative consequences rather than differences in expected benefits.

Moreover, recent research on expectancies has been focused on the development and refinement of instruments to measure drug expectancies (Corbin, Morean and Benedict, 2008; Reig-Ferrer and Cepeda-Benito, 2006; Rohsenow et al., 2005). In Spain, Reig-Ferrer and Cepeda-Benito (2006) have analysed the factor structure of smoking expectancies, in daily smokers and those who have never smoked, using the Smoking Consequences Questionnaire. The data gave support to an eight-factor structure of the Smoking Consequences Questionnaire-Spanish in the sample of daily smokers (namely, negative effect reduction; stimulation/state enhancement; health risk; taste/sensor-motor manipulation; social facilitation; weight control; craving/addiction; and boredom reduction). In addition, the Positive Drinking Consequences Questionnaire (Corbin, Morean and Benedict, 2008) was recently developed as a valid and reliable measure of positive drinking consequences.

3. Conclusions

Although significant progress has been made in recent years in drug research, a number of issues still need further clarification.

As regards research on impulsivity, if it is now well established that chronic abuse of drugs is associated with significant deficits in response inhibition and decision making (and other executive functions), future studies need to address the underlying mechanisms of this neurocognitive profile. For example, is there any relationship between impulsivity and orbitofrontal cortex lesions? In fact, recent research has demonstrated that the orbitofrontal cortex is involved in decision making as well as evaluation and inhibition of stimulus-reward associations (Verdejo-Garcia et al., 2006b).

It is also important to consider that some theoretical explanations still tend to obscure the conceptual differences between sensation seeking and impulsivity. Although some progress has been made, the conclusions of the present review also raise the issue of whether sensation seeking and impulsivity are unique constructs or facets of a behavioural disinhibition trait. At least one study, conducted by Magid, MacLean and Colder (2007) found that impulsivity and sensation seeking "are differentially related to alcohol use and alcohol-related problems, such that impulsivity is more strongly related to alcohol problems, whereas sensation seeking is more strongly related to alcohol use" (p. 2058).

Indices of impulsivity and sensation seeking among drug-dependent individuals may be affected by several mediating variables. For example, Vassileva and colleagues (2007), examining the influence of impulsivity, found that antisocial behaviour was associated with better cognitive impulse control, independent of the extent of polysubstance involvement. However, this issue still represents an important limitation of the research on personality traits and drug abuse.

Finally, expectancy and personality traits are usually described as competing constructs in drug-abuse prediction. Although some attempts have been made to integrate these constructs in a coherent conceptual model of drug-abuse prediction and risk (for example, An-Ting Fu et al., 2007; Hendershot et al., 2007; Leventhal and Schmitz, 2006), future studies need to clarify better the nature of the causal relationship between personality traits and cognitive constructs such as expectancies.

References

Alessio, M., Balocco, R. and Laghi, R. (2006), "The problem of binge drinking among Italian university students: a preliminary investigation", *Addictive Behaviors*, 31, 2328-2333.

Andrew, M. and Cronin, C. (1997), "Two measures of sensation seeking as predictors of alcohol use among high school males", *Personality and Individual Differences*, 22, 393-401.

Anestis, M., Selby, E. and Joiner, E. (2007), "The role of urgency in maladaptive behaviours", *Behavior Research and Therapy*, 45, 3018-3029.

An-Ting Fu, Huei-Chen Ko, Jo Yung-Wei Wu, Bing-Lin Cherng and Chung-Ping Cheng (2007), "Impulsivity and expectancy in risk for alcohol use: comparing male and female college students in Taiwan", *Addictive Behaviors*, 32, 1887-1896.

Ballaz, S., Akil, H. and Watson, S. (2007a), "The 5-HT7 receptor: role in novel object discrimination and relation to novelty-seeking behavior", *Neuroscience*, 149, 192-202.

Ballaz, S., Akil, H. and Watson, S. (2007b), "Analysis of 5-HT6 and 5-HT7 receptor gene expression in rats showing differences in novelty-seeking behavior", *Neuroscience*, 147, 428-438.

Billieux, J., Lindena, M. and Ceschia, G. (2006), "Which dimensions of impulsivity are related to cigarette craving?", *Addictive Behaviors*, 32, 1189-1199.

Clark, L., Robbins, T., Ersche, K. and Shaakian, B. (2006), "Reflection impulsivity in current and former substance users", *Biological Psychiatry*, 60, 515-522.

Conway, K.P., Kane, R.J., Ball, S.A., Poling, J.C. and Rounsaville, B.J. (2003), "Personality, substance of choice, and polysubstance involvement among substance dependent patients", *Drug and Alcohol Dependence*, 71, 65-75.

Corbin, W., Morean, M. and Benedict, D. (2008), "The positive drinking questionnaire (PDCQ): validation of a new assessment tool", *Addictive Behaviors*, 33, 56-68.

Dafters, R. (2005), "Impulsivity, inhibition and negative priming in ecstasy users", *Addictive Behaviors*, 31, 1436-1441.

Demmel, R., Nicolai, J. and Gregorzik, S. (2006), "Alcohol expectancies and current mood state in social drinkers", *Addictive Behaviors*, 31, 859-867.

Dom, G., Wilde, B., Hulstijn, W. and Sabbe, B. (2006), "Dimensions of impulsive behavior in alcoholics", *Personality and Individual Differences,* 42, 465-476.

Doran, N., McChargue, D. and Spring, B. (2008), "Effect of impulsivity on cardiovascular and subjective reactivity to smoking cues", *Addictive Behaviors,* 33, 167-172.

Fisher, S. and Smith, G. (2007), "Binge eating, problem drinking, and pathological gambling: linking behavior to shared traits and social learning", *Personality and Individual Differences* (article in press, corrected proof).

Gaher, R. and Simons, J. (2007), "Evaluations and expectancies of alcohol and marijuana problems among college students", *Psychology of Addictive Behaviors,* 21, 545-554.

Gurpegui, M., Jurado, D., Luna, J., Fernandez-Molina, C. et al. (2007), "Personality traits associated with caffeine intake and smoking", *Progress in Neuro-Psychopharmacology & Biological Psychiatry,* 31, 997-1005.

Hayaki, J., Anderson, B. and Stein, M. (2007), "Drug use expectancies among non abstinent cocaine users", *Drug and Alcohol Dependence* (article in press, corrected proof).

Hendershot, C., Stoner, S., George, W. and Norris, J. (2007), "Alcohol use, expectancies, and sexual sensation seeking as correlates of HIV risk behavior in heterosexual young adults", *Psychology of Addictive Behaviors,* 21, 365-372.

Hittner, J. and Swickert, R. (2006), "Sensation seeking and alcohol use: a meta-analytic review", *Addictive Behaviors,* 31, 1383-1401.

Legrand, F., Goma-i-freixanet, M., Kaltenbach, M. and Joly, P. (2007), "Association between sensation seeking and alcohol consumption in French college students: some ecological data collected in 'open bar' parties", *Personality and Individual Differences,* 43, 1950-1959.

Lejuez, C., Bornovalova, M., Reynolds, E., Daughters, S. and Curtin, J. (2007), "Risk factors in the relationship between gender and crack/cocaine", *Experimental and Clinical Psychopharmacology,* 15, 165-175.

Leventhal, A. and Schmitz (2006), "The role of drug use outcome expectancies in substance abuse risk: an interactional–transformational model", *Addictive Behaviors,* 31, 2038-2062.

Lundahl, L. and Lukas, S. (2006), "Negative cocaine effect expectancies are associated with subjective response to cocaine challenge in recreational cocaine users", *Addictive Behaviors,* 32, 1262-1271.

Magid, V. and Colder, C. (2007), "The UPPS impulsive behavior scale: factor structure and associations with college drinking", *Personality and Individual Differences,* 43, 1927-1937.

Magid, V., MacLean, M. and Colder, C. (2007), "Differentiating between sensation seeking and impulsivity through mediated relations with alcohol use problems", *Addictive Behaviors,* 32, 2046-2061.

Negreiros, J. (2006), *Psychological drug research: current themes and future developments*, Strasbourg: Council of Europe Publishing.

Oswald, L., Wong, D., Zhou, Y., Kumar, A., Brasic, J., Alexander, M., Ye, W., Kuwabara, H., Hilton, J. and Wand, G. (2007), "Impulsivity and chronic stress are associated with amphetamine-induced striatal dopamine release", *Neuroimage,* 36, 153-166.

Reig-Ferrer, A. and Cepeda-Benito, A. (2006), "Smoking expectancies in smokers and never smokers: an examination of the Smoking Consequences Questionnaire-Spanish", *Addictive Behaviors,* 32, 1405-1415.

Rohsenow, D., Colby, S., Martin, R. and Monti, P. (2005), "Nicotine and other substance interaction expectancies questionnaire: relationship of expectancies to substance use", *Addictive Behaviors,* 30, 629-641.

Ryb, G.E. et al. (2006). "Risk perception and impulsivity: Association with risky behaviours and substance abuse disorders", *Accident Analysis & Prevention*, 3, 567-573.

Simmons, J. and Arens, A. (2007), "Moderating effects of sensitivity to punishment and sensitivity to reward on associations between marijuana effect expectancies and use", *Psychology of Addictive Behaviours,* 21, 409-414.

Stansfield, K. and Kirstein, C. (2007), "Chronic cocaine or ethanol exposure during adolescence alters novelty-related behaviors in adulthood", *Pharmacology, Biochemistry and Behavior,* 86, 637-642.

Vassileva, J., Gonzalez, R., Bechara, A. and Martin, E. (2007), "Are all drug addicts impulsive? Effects of antisociality and extent of multidrug use on cognitive and motor impulsivity", *Addictive Behaviors*, 32, 3071-3076.

Verdejo-Garcia, A., Bechara, A., Recknor, E. and Pérez-Garcia, M. (2007), "Negative emotion-driven impulsivity predicts substance dependence problems", *Drug and Alcohol Dependence*, 91, 213-219.

Verdejo-Garcia, A., Perales, J. and Pérez-Garcia, M. (2006a), "Cognitive impulsivity in cocaine and heroin polysubstance abusers", *Addictive Behaviors,* 32, 950-966.

Verdejo-Garcia, A., Rivas-Péres, C., Vilar-López, R. and Pérez-Garcia, M. (2006b), "Strategic self-regulation, decision-making and emotion processing in poly-substance abusers in their first year of abstinence", *Drug and Alcohol Dependence,* 86, 139-146.

Watson, D. and Clark, L.A. (1993), "Behavioural disinhibition versus constraint: a dispositional perspective", in Wegner, D.M. and Pennebaker, J.W. (eds), *Handbook of mental control*, Englewood Cliffs, NJ: Prentice Hall.

Whiteside, S. and Lynam, D. (2001), "The five factor model of impulsivity: using a structural model of personality to understand impulsivity", *Personality and Individual Differences,* 30, 669-689.

Chapter 3 – Drug research: recent signals from the biomedical field

by Professor Richard Muscat, Department of Biomedical Sciences, University of Malta

1. Introduction

In 2006, the Research Platform of the Council of Europe's Pompidou Group published *Biomedical research in the drugs field: current themes, new methodologies, developments and considerations* (ISBN: 92-871-6017-1). This paper is an attempt to update current thinking. In effect, this time round we will mainly focus on an update of the current hypothesis for initial drug use, and the models for the switch to dependence/addiction in a minority of individuals who go on using drugs. Both the genetic predisposition to develop substance dependence and the latest information on drug relapse will also be taken into account.

The rationale for adopting this approach is that this information should be readily available to those on the front-line treating individuals with substance dependence. Moreover, medications for this disorder are limited to the opiates, nicotine and alcohol, whereas no such agents exist for cocaine, amphetamines or marijuana.

From the standpoint of society, such information should also be readily available to policy makers and the public alike, as it is both these groups who have the possibility to shape policy, especially in relation to treatment.

Thus this update will take on the following format: firstly, the clinical manifestations of substance dependence are highlighted; secondly, current theories are re-visited as well as those related to relapse; thirdly, there is a brief account of the genetic factors that influence predisposition to drug use as well as those that play a role in the development and maintenance of drug dependence; and, finally, there is a concluding section.

2. Clinical manifestations of drug dependence/addiction

From a clinical perspective, it has been suggested by Goodman (2008), based on his clinical experience with a number of patients with substance dependence, that 10 characteristic features seem to abound in this cohort. In the first instance, the illness tends to occur in adolescence or early adulthood, it is also characterised by a narrowing of the behavioural repertoire and common subjective experiences, such as elation and craving, and it develops over time with certain behaviours becoming more frequent at the expense of others.

Tolerance, withdrawal and relapse are also prime characteristics, as well as neglect and recurrent themes, such as denial and rationalisation.

The presence of substance dependence is also associated with affective disorders, anxiety disorders, attention deficit disorder and personality disorders, and is more likely to abound in this cohort than in the general population. Major depression, anxiety and personality disorders are thus found more commonly among those with substance dependence than would be found in the population at large (Couwenbergh et al., 2006; Ross, Glaser and Germanson, 1988; Merikangas et al., 1998).

In addition, Goodman in his review also highlighted that those diagnosed with substance dependence are more at risk than the general population of developing a related addictive disorder at some point in their lifetime. Moreover, first-degree relatives are also at greater risk than the general population of developing an addictive disorder, which includes substance dependence.

In relation to what comes first, the psychiatric disorder or substance dependence, it has been demonstrated that the former predates the latter by typically between five to 10 years (Couwenbergh et al., 2006; Shaffer and Eber, 2002). It has also been reported by the WHO that there were significant predictive associations between primary mental disorders, and first substance use and dependency among problem drug users. However, to all intents and purposes, it would appear that anxiety disorders, and to a lesser extent depression, precede and increase the risk of substance use.

Personality traits also appear to increase the risk of developing substance dependence, and of these impulsivity, sensation seeking, risk taking, low stress tolerance and nonconformity normally predate substance use. A more detailed overview of personality traits and their relation to substance dependence can be found in the chapter on the psychological update. However, information on the genetics of impulsivity and its relation to substance dependence can be found below.

Thus, from the account of the clinical features of substance dependence, it would appear that the behaviours that result from such may arise in part as a consequence of problems in cognitive and neurobiological function that precede their onset. It may thus be inferred that substance dependence does not arise as a result of the lifestyle that may be attributed to the syndrome, but from some underlying neurobiological dysfunction.

3. Current theories in the neuroscience of drug dependence/addiction

Since 2006 most theories in this field have addressed particular issues and have attempted to include in their models the major criteria for drug dependence/addiction, namely the increased motivation to acquire the drug of abuse, the increase in effort to seek the drug and continued drug use irrespective of the aversive consequences. Moreover, it is now acknowledged that at best only 20 % (Anthony, Warner and Kessler, 1994) of those who use drugs go on to become dependent, and this factor has also been incorporated into the models addressing drug dependence/addiction.

In the first of the theories to be expounded in this field since 2006, Everitt and his colleagues (2008) suggested that drug dependence/addiction results as a consequence of repeated drug use and the strengthening of the circuits in the brain involved in habit formation. Thus, compulsive drug use as is the case in addiction arises from a series of steps or conditions that alters the striatal circuitry to give rise to the aberrant behaviour observed in the clinic. The major leap forward from their stance in 2006 is the fact that initiation of drug use is under the control, in the main, of the ventral striatum, and most notably the nucleus accumbens core region, which processes information related to motivation/reward, but with repetitive use of the drug over a sustained period of time the maintenance or the switch to drug dependence/addiction occurs as the dorsal striatum takes over, which is primarily involved in the selection of action.

In addition, they also go on to suggest that the trait of impulsivity also increases the likelihood of the addiction and relapse. They argue that from their findings in laboratory rats, in which such may be selected following exposure to a behavioural task that involves withholding of a response, these animals went on to learn to administer cocaine as did the control group but they then take on board more and more of the drug unlike their counterparts. It was also shown that these rats also have low D2 receptor availability in the nucleus accumbens, as do human drug addicts (Volkow, Fowler and Wang, 2004) even when abstinent (Volkow and Wise, 2005). Thus impulsivity per se may predispose one to use drugs in the first place and then facilitate the switch between occasional use and drug dependency/addiction and finally also render abstinent addicts more susceptible to relapse.

Unlike Everitt and his colleagues who support the notion that compulsive habit formation through the dorsal striatum is the mechanism responsible for sustaining drug use in dependence/addiction, Robinson and Berridge (2008) propose that the increase in responsiveness of the ventral striatum gives rise to the increased motivation or increased wanting of drugs in the dependent subject. Their argument runs along the lines that with increased use of drugs over a period of time, the response to the drug effect becomes sensitised or increased with regard to the stimuli that accompany drug use and thus they become progressively more relevant at the expense of the rewarding aspects per se. Moreover, such conditioned stimuli can be shown to exert their effects in a number of rat models, as well as in humans presented with such images while undergoing positron emission tomography (PET) imaging. The "wanting' over "liking" highlights the incentive sensisation theory for drug addiction, but the authors have now also added that cortical dysfunction may also play a role in poor decision making and loss of inhibitory control as witnessed in drug dependents. As a result, drug dependency/addiction may be viewed as a condition in which the bias for drug-related stimuli has been amplified and "gives impulsive drug wanting a life of its own" (Robinson and Berridge, 2003).

On the contrary, Koob and Le Moal (2008) suggest that in dependency/addiction, it is the reward part of the equation that has been altered and not per se the wanting, even though this is also engaged, for example, in relapse. They have previously suggested that with repeated drug use, a tolerance to the rewarding or pleasurable effects sets in and in an attempt to overcome the tolerance further drug use follows to try and obtain the original effect. Further elaboration of this concept engaged the idea that on stopping the drug the individual would go into a state of dysphoria, rather than euphoria, as a result of the tolerance or greater impact of stimuli required to stimulate the reward system. Thus, to offset this condition, the drug user seeks to obtain and take on board more of the drug, thus setting up a sequence of events that gives rise to compulsive drug use. In their latest updated model for drug dependency/addiction, they invoke an opponent process model that takes into account both the reward and anti-reward systems to explain the condition. In effect, they suggest that as with all body systems under homeostatic control, that is mechanisms present to counteract any changes in set point, drug addiction is a dysregulation of the homeostatic system of brain reward. More so, as it is an aberrant allostatic response which is the culprit. This comes into play on occasions when stability is required, for example when changes are occurring, and thus provides the ability to re-set the set point for a time in the face of adversity. With repeated drug use, this response becomes the modus operandi and can be considered as the basis for compulsive drug taking.

Tassin (2008) has been conducting a series of experiments in which he has used the sensitisation model of addiction to determine the underlying neurobiological components that give rise to such a phenomena. He has argued that the increase in dopamine function said to occur in the incentive sensitisation model put forward by Robinson and Berridge is in effect caused by upstream effects in the noradrenergic and serotonergic neurotransmitter systems. Moreover, these systems that arise from cell bodies in subcortical structures and terminate in the cortex are thought to stimulate the excitatory neurotransmitter glutamate, which in turn excites the dopamine cells in the meso-limbic forebrain. Moreover, the two systems seem to interact with one another at a subcortical level in that the noradrenergic system on activation stimulates the serotonergic system, which in turn inhibits the noradrenergic system. It is also understood that the role of the noradrenergic system per se is to provide better processing of an external stimulus by focusing attention, whereas the serotonergic system provides the damper on this effect to protect the system from too intense stimuli. Thus, with repeated drug use, it is suggested that this coupling mechanism is disturbed, with the result that the noradrenergic system is allowed free reign to run, which would account for the increased vigilance to drug stimuli, as posited by Robinson and Berridge, and also for the long-term changes in brain circuitry associated with dependence/addiction.

From the point of view of the molecular mechanism that provides the switch from occasional drug use to compulsive drug use and the maintenance of such, Hyman and Nestler (2001) have suggested that Delta FosB may be a prime candidate. It has been demonstrated that this protein is increased following the intake of any type of drug of abuse and more importantly it is stimulated following repeated use, and thus the response does not adapt or habituate and hence may be the molecule that enables the transition to long-term sensitisation of the striatal dopamine function. This particular protein is synthesised from the activation of what is known as an immediate early gene – namely, c-fos gene – following drug stimulation, and in turn the product of this gene, Delta FosB, may switch on or off conventional genes that may be responsible for the long-term effects associated with chronic drug use. Nestler now makes the point that Delta FosB may provide a marker of the activation state of the reward pathway, and thus this may provide some insight into the state of play in an individual chronically using drugs or in one who is in treatment. Finally, he also speculates how it would be advantageous if one were to discover a chemical that may be used with imaging techniques, such as PET, in which the levels of Delta FosB could be monitored, for example during treatment.

Relapse is also another important aspect of the drug cycle, especially with regard to treatment and thus this field of study has received much attention of late. Stewart (2008) has used the reinstatement model of relapse to seek answers to questions such as:

(A) What are the primary triggers for relapse?

(B) What brain systems underpin these effects?

(C) What is the basis for the maintenance of vulnerability to relapse?

In their model, animals are trained to a press a lever in which access to the drug of abuse is made available with accompanying stimuli, such as a light or tone, on the delivery of the drug. Following steady state responding, which is achieved over a significant period of time, to mimic the state of chronicity, a period of extinction is enforced in which animals are exposed to the same conditions but drug delivery is withheld. To evaluate the effects of conditioned stimuli, stress and priming, animals are reintroduced to the environment in which they learnt to take on board the drug of abuse. In the first instance, the effects of conditioned stimuli are examined by testing how willing the animals are to start responding again to the drug-associated lever. It is apparent that those exposed to such a previous pairing will start to respond to the lever pretty quickly and this is said to be a demonstration of the impact of the cues to reinstate responding, even though drug delivery was not made available. The same occurs if the subjects are exposed to some form of mild stress or a very low dose of the drug used as a primer. Thus, conditioned cues, stress and priming doses of the drug of abuse all reinstate responding or cause relapse. Moreover, it is stated that the brain areas responsible for such effects all converge on a common pathway, namely the medial prefrontal cortex and its output to the mesolimbic dopamine system. Maintenance of such is suggested to arise from the sensitisation of the mesolimbic system, as posited by Robinson and Berridge (1993) and outlined above.

Shaham (2008) has also used the reinstatement model of relapse in his studies, although in this instance the overall context under which the drug is taken on board is the main focus of his series of studies on relapse. In this case, the reinstatement model is also used but the training schedule is different in one respect, namely that subjects undergoing extinction do so in a different environment or context. Once again, following extinction when animals are reintroduced to the same context in which they received the drug, they start responding again to the drug lever even though this does not result in drug delivery. The brain circuit and the mechanism for such is suggested to arise from the frontal cortex and ventral tegmental area, in which glutamatergic and dopamine neurons arising from each are said to activate the ventral striatum in firing mode. In addition, but unlike the circuit said to be responsible for the enabling of conditioned or discrete cues, the hippocampus and its input to the ventral striatum is said to be important as regards signalling context. Finally, these results may have some importance in relation to the treatment of drug addiction in the clinic, in that invoking abstinence in the patient may be regarded as the period of extinction and this like the studies cited above occurs in a different environment to which drug taking has occurred. Thus, it may be prudent to attempt to prevent relapse following the patients discharge to the home environment by introducing other rewards other than the drug during abstinence or that abstinence occurs in a number of different contexts or environments.

4. Genetics of drug dependence/addiction

It is now understood that dependence/addiction or the vulnerability to develop this disorder is influenced by the type of genes we inherit from our parents. That is not to say that the social context does not have a say in the development of dependence/addiction, but genetic heritability is of the order of some 50% independent of the substance in question. It may be higher for specific substances, such as heroin, which is reported to be in the region of 70%.

Recent studies in this field have suggested that dependence/addiction is heterogeneous from a genetic standpoint, as well as polygenic. This implies that in the first instance, a set number of genes acting independently may together produce vulnerability to dependence. However, it would appear that this provides only a small propensity to develop dependence whereas polygenicity would appear to be the main factor. In this case, there are a number of genes acting in concert to produce the vulnerability with no single gene responsible on its own. In light of these findings, it has been proposed that it may prove to be more fruitful to examine the genetic influence on a particular feature or trait that has a corresponding biological substrate and thus be able to account for the single genes responsible. This has also proved to be challenging except for example in the case of some particular sub-typing with respect to alcohol. Thus this sub-typing of alcohol dependence has produced a more homogenous grouping and thus reduced the overall number of characteristics that may be attributed to this disorder (Wong and Schumann, 2008).

As was predicted, the way forward was the use of genome-wide association studies to counter the limitations of single-candidate gene studies. This involves scanning the whole genome or the entire complement of genetic material that sits on our 23 chromosomes through the use of novel technology known as micro-arrays. Uhl and colleagues (2008) have used such a technique to look for any genetic variation among different populations, namely, European-American, Asians and European per se with addiction/dependency to different substances, alcohol, methamphetamine and nicotine. They found in comparison to the control groups that independent of substances there were a number of genetic variations that could be grouped to provide an association with dependence/addiction. There are a number and include genes that are involved in forming neuronal connections, enzymatic activity as well as ion channels and transport processes. Importantly, they are all expressed in the brain but the surprise here is the fact that a number of genes that turned up were responsible for forming nerve cell connections during development and they are expressed in brain areas related to memory formation, such as the hippocampus. In light of the discussion above on drug relapse, it is then hardly surprising to find that the propensity for relapse in recovered addicts persists for a significant number of years.

Lately, it has been suggested that impulse control disorders resemble addictions and some have even gone as far as stating that these disorders may be considered addictions (Brewer and Potenza, 2008). Impulse control disorders are said to fall somewhere along the impulsive–compulsive continuum. They include pathological gambling and kleptomania amongst others and are thus repetitive and usually pleasurable. Impulsivity per se may be a key factor in a number of psychiatric disorders, including impulse control disorders and addiction/dependence. Some characteristics of impulsivity, as described in the previous chapter in this overview (Negreiros), include lack of premeditation and sensation seeking, but key to its resemblance to that of dependence/addiction is the definition given by Moeller and colleagues (2001), "a predisposition to rapid unplanned reactions … with diminished regard to negative consequences …". From a genetic standpoint, it is also uncanny that that family and twin studies account for up to 60 % of the variance for risk of dependency/addiction (Kreek et al., 2005). In relation to specific factors, it would appear that the reduction in availability in dopamine D2 receptors in human and animal studies provides a basis for a possible mechanism for both impulsivity and the development of addiction/dependence.

5. Conclusions

From a clinical perspective it would now appear that we have a good understanding of the criteria that may define substance dependence, and this in turn has enabled better models of dependence/addiction to be implemented that take into account the phenomena in question.

At present there are three models that are worthy of note in the field of neuroscience that attempt to explain the process of dependence/addiction and the underlying neurobiological substrates. These in turn are:

– the habitual or compulsive model of addiction;

– the incentive sensitisation model of addiction;

– the aberrant allostatic model.

Moreover, the molecule suggested to provide the switch to addiction is said to be Delta FosB; its activation in turn enables the mesolimbic dopamine system, also known as the ventral striatum, to remain in a state of what is known as "long-term sensitisation".

The genes now thought to be involved with a predisposition to drug dependence are large in number and would appear to act in concert to provide vulnerability, with no one gene being able to do so alone. Genes involved with connectivity of the nervous system in the brain and thus also with the means through which memories are formed are also thought to be involved in the addiction process, and hence they are likely to increase the propensity for relapse.

6. Glossary

Allostasis

The concept of allostasis was proposed by Sterling and Eyer in 1988 to describe an additional process of re-establishing homeostasis or stability, but one that responds to a challenge instead of the normal subtle ebb and flow of bodily functions.

Gene

The basic unit of heredity; a section of DNA coding for a particular trait.

Immediate early gene

These are genes that are activated transiently and rapidly in response to a wide variety of cellular stimuli and are distinct from late onset genes, which are only activated by the products of these immediate early genes. It may also describe cellular proteins that are made immediately following stimulation of a resting cell by extracellular signals.

Neurotransmitter

A chemical such as noradrenaline and serotonin, which is released at synapses – namely, the gap between nerve cells – to mediate signalling between such nerve cells.

Polygenic inheritance

Refers to inheritance of a phenotypic characteristic (trait) that is attributable to two or more genes and their interaction with the environment. Many genes are responsible for determining a number of a person's characteristics, so modifying only one of those genes only slightly changes the appearance of the trait. Many disorders with genetic components are polygenic, including autism, cancer, diabetes and numerous others. Most phenotypic characteristics are the result of the interaction of multiple genes.

Positron emission tomography (PET)

A brain imaging technique that may be used to monitor nerve cell activity through the use of radioactive substances. In effect, PET maps the distribution of radioactive labelled substances that have been injected intravenously into the subject. These substances emit positively charged particles which collide with negatively charged ones, resulting in the release of energy, which is detected and visualised as a colour image on a monitor.

Receptor

Refers to a specialised molecule within or on the surface of a cell that serves as a recognition or binding site for neurotransmitters, antigens, antibodies, or other cellular or immunological components. This selective binding causes a change in the activity of the cell.

Sensitisation

The process by which a behavioural response to a stimulus increases in intensity, frequency or duration even though the stimulus per se has not altered.

Striatum

A subcortical structure made up of a ventral and dorsal part, which processes information related to motivation/reward with regard to the former, and in the latter case information related to the selection of the most appropriate action in order to achieve the required goal. It appears stripped in brain sections, thus its name.

Synapse

A specialised structure or junction between nerve cells through which a signal is transmitted, usually via a neurotransmitter, from one nerve cell to another.

References

Anthony, J.C., Warner, L.A. and Kessler, R.C. (1994), "Comparative epidemiology of dependence on tobacco, alcohol, controlled substances and inhalants: basic findings from the National Comorbidity Survey", *Experimental Clinical Psychopharmacology*, 2, 244-268.

Brewer, J.A. and Potenza M.N. (2008), "The neurobiology and genetics of impulse control disorders: relationship to drug addictions", *Biochemical Pharmacology*, 75, 63-75.

Couwenbergh, C., van den Brink, W., Zwart, K., Vreugdenhil, C., van Wijngaarden-Cremers, P. and van der Gaag, R.J. (2006), "Comorbid psychopathology in adolescents and young adults treated for substance use disorders", *European Child Adolescent Psychiatry*, 15, 319-328.

Crombag, H.S., Bossert, J.M., Koya, E. and Shaham, Y. (2008), "Context-induced relapse to drug seeking: a review", *Philosophical Transactions of the Royal Society*, B, 3233-3243.

Everitt, B.J., Belin, D., Economidou, D., Pelloux, Y., Dalley, J.W. and Robbins, T.W. (2008), "Neural mechanisms underlying the vulnerability to develop compulsive drug seeking habits and addiction", *Philosophical Transactions of the Royal Society*, B, 363, 3125-3135.

Goodman, A. (2008), "Neurobiology of addiction: an integrative review", *Biochemical Pharmacology*, 75, 266-322.

Hyman, S.E. and Malenka, R.C. (2001), "Addiction and the brain: the neurobiology of compulsion and its persistence", *Nature Neuroscience Reviews*, 2, 695-703.

Koob, G.F. and Le Moal, M. (2008), "Neurobiological mechanisms for opponent motivational processes in addiction", *Philosophical Transactions of the Royal Society*, B, 363, 3113-3123.

Kreek, M.J., Nielsen, D.A., Butelman, E.R. and Laforge, K.S. (2005), "Genetic influences on impulsivity, risk taking, stress responsivity and vulnerability to drug abuse and addiction", *Nature Neuroscience*, 8, 1450-1457.

Merikangas, K.R., Mehta, R.L., Molnar, B.E., Walters, E.E., Swendsen, J.D. and Aguilar-Gaziola, S. (1998), "Comorbidity of substance use disorders with mood and anxiety disorders: results of the International Consortium in Psychiatric Epidemiology", *Addictive Behaviors*, 23, 893-907.

Moeller, P.G., Barratt, E.S., Dougherty, D.M., Schmitz, J.M. and Swann, A.C. (2001), "Psychiatric aspects of impulsivity", *American Journal of Psychiatry*, 158, 1783-1793.

Muscat, R. (2006), *Biomedical research in the drugs field: current themes, new methodologies, developments and considerations*, Strasbourg: Council of Europe Publishing.

Nestler, E.J. (2008), "Transcriptional mechanisms of addiction: role of delta FosB", *Philosophical Transactions of the Royal Society*, B, 3245-3255.

Robinson, T.E. and Berridge, K.C. (1993), "The neural basis of drug craving: an incentive-sensitization theory of addiction", *Brain Research Reviews*, 18, 247-291.

Robinson, T.E. and Berridge, K.C. (2003), "Addiction", *Annual Review of Psychology*, 54, 25-53.

Robinson, T.E. and Berridge, K.C. (2008), "The incentive sensitization theory of addiction: some current issues", *Philosophical Transactions of the Royal Society*, B, 3137- 3146.

Ross, H.E., Glaser, F.B. and Germanson, T. (1988), "The prevalence of psychiatric disorders in patients with alcohol and other drug problems", *Archives of General Psychiatry*, 45, 1023-1031.

Shaffer, H.J. and Eber, G.B. (2002), "Temporal progression of cocaine dependence symptoms in the US National Comorbidity Survey", *Addiction*, 97, 543-554.

Shaffer, H.J. and Korn, D.A. (2002), "Gambling and related mental disorders: a public health analysis", *Annual Reviews of Public Health*, 23, 171-212.

Stewart, J. (2008), "Psychological and neural mechanisms of relapse", *Philosophical Transactions of the Royal Society*, B, 3147-3158.

Tassin, J.-P. (2008), "Uncoupling between noradrenergic and serotonergic neurons as a molecular basis of stable changes in behavior induced by repeated drugs of abuse", *Biochemical Pharmacology*, 75, 85-97.

Uhl, G.R., Drgon, T., Johnson, C., Fatusin, O.O., Liu, Q.R., Contoreggi, C., Li, C.Y., Buck, K. and Crabbe, J. (2008), "'Higher order' addiction molecular genetics: convergent data from genome-wide association in humans and mice", *Biochemical Pharmacology*, 75, 98-111.

Volkow, N.D., Fowler, J.S. and Wang, G.J. (2004), "The addicted human brain viewed in the light of imaging studies: brain circuits and treatment strategies", *Neuropharmacology*, 27, 3-13.

Volkow, N.D. and Wise, R.A. (2005), "How can drug addiction help us understand obesity?", *Nature Neuroscience*, 8, 555-560.

Wong, C.C.Y. and Schumann, G. (2008), "Genetics of addictions: strategies for addressing heterogeneity and polygenicity of substance use disorders", *Philosophical Transactions of the Royal Society*, B, 3213-3222.

Chapter 4 – Initial assessment of the European Scientific Conference on "How can we better treat drug addiction? New scientific and clinical challenges for Europe"

9 and 10 December 2008

Grand Amphithéâtre of the Sorbonne, Paris

by Dominique Vuillaume, Joint Ministerial Task Force for Combating Drugs and Drug Addiction (MILDT), Paris

This conference was one of three events organised in the second half of 2008 by the French Interdepartmental Mission for the Fight against Drugs and Drug Addiction (MILDT) in the context of the French presidency of the European Union.

The aim of this scientific meeting was to provide an update on the most recent advances in research on understanding the mechanisms of drug addiction in order to identify promising courses of action with regard to both the care of drug-dependent people and new information, prevention and reintegration strategies that could be considered by the authorities.

From the outset, the conference organisers had adopted an open European approach, since 14 scientists out of the 25 speakers were from different European countries (the United Kingdom, Germany, Italy, Spain, Switzerland, Belgium), one was from the United States and four others represented the various European institutions (European Commission with representatives of DG Sanco and DG Justice; the Council of Europe's Pompidou Group through its Research Platform, and the European Monitoring Centre for Drugs and Drug Addiction).

The conference's seven theme-based sessions (see the attached programme) were introduced by Robert West, editor-in-chief of the magazine *Addiction* (London), an authoritative international scientific magazine in this field of research.

1. Challenges and problems considered at the conference

In many countries, drug abuse and/or addiction is a major public health problem because of its repercussions in terms of harm to health (premature disease and death) and social damage (accident proneness, criminality associated with the acquisition of illegal drugs, losses of production and income).

Apart from the 8 million tobacco-dependent individuals in France, there are some 5 million heavy drinkers (2 million of whom are alcohol dependent), 550 000 daily cannabis users and about 150 000 people who are heavily opiate dependent. At the same time, there has been a rapid increase in the consumption of cocaine in the last few years, which is reflected in a strong rise in demand for treatment for those dependent on this substance. The same trends can be broadly observed at the European level, as evidenced by the latest epidemiological data provided by the European Monitoring Centre for Drugs and Drug Addiction (EMCDDA).

While significant progress has been made in dealing with some of these addictions (nicotine replacement therapy and new pharmacological complexes for tobacco addiction, drug replacement therapy for heroin addiction), clinicians still face major difficulties regarding other forms of addiction, such as cocaine use, alcohol dependence or heavy cannabis use by some teenagers and young adults, not to mention multiple drug use and multiple addiction, which are becoming increasingly frequent among heavy drug users and pose virtually insoluble problems in terms of treatment strategy for clinicians working in the field.

Given this situation, the development of research on abuse and addiction is a real priority, especially on the clinical aspect. As the President of the MILDT, Mr Etienne Apaire, pointed out in the opening session of the conference, "the treatment of people dependent on drugs remains by definition a vexed question because of the diversity of patient profiles and expectations, the psychiatric disorders often associated with addictive behaviour, situations of multiple addiction that are sometimes inextricably linked to one another and the availability of ample supplies of substances, which multiplies the chances of a relapse". As a result, it is difficult to carry out research on the treatment of addiction, especially clinical research: it is not easy to form homogeneous groups of patients to evaluate treatments, there are a significant number of "lost to follow-up" patients in the studies because treatment is frequently discontinued, and it is difficult at the preclinical stage to develop animal models of the addiction that come convincingly close to the conditions prevailing in humans. Moreover, there are many different factors involved in the processes that lead to addiction and this calls for interdisciplinary scientific research that is by its very nature complex and hard to devise and implement.

Still in the opening session, the French Minister for Health, Roselyne Bachelot, reminded participants of the issues involved in the development of clinical research on addictions: "The aim is to improve the quality of professional practices and training … in order to ensure better care for dependent people. At present, the risks associated with the consumption of cocaine are underestimated, and arrangements for the care and treatment of regular users of the substance are still poorly regulated because no treatment protocol has been validated".

Professor Robert West, the last speaker in the opening session, expressed his conviction that the question of understanding addiction went hand in hand with understanding human behaviour, and pointed out that the purely pharmacological effect of a substance was not enough to explain addiction, as had been believed in the 19th century, when people had referred to morphine addiction and, a little later, to drug addiction. Similarly, environmental factors alone could not account for the process leading to addiction. Addiction was first and foremost a form of behaviour that was maintained despite the problems it caused for the person concerned and for others. When we spoke of addiction, it was very important to understand that it was a question of an imbalance between "a strength of motivation to indulge in heavy consumption" and the potentially weak influence of competing motivations that might counterbalance it. What we did at every moment was "determined by the strongest of competing impulses and inhibitions". Dependent individuals often had very low levels of competing motivation and/or a low capacity for inhibition. Drawing on this conceptual framework, Professor West proposed the EPICURE model for intervention in the case of addictive behaviour. This model comprises seven dimensions: E for education to "promote a greater understanding of the harms of existing behaviour and benefits of change"; P for persuasion, involving the presentation of "images and arguments that turn understanding into feelings of want or need to change"; I for inducement, which consists in "introducing additional positive rewards for change" (such as shopping vouchers); C for coercion, by which he means the fear of sanctions associated with the acquisition of drugs and the possible modification of the consumer's assessment of the benefit-risk balance; U for upskilling, which means the acquisition of personal resources to control the craving and implement the decision to change existing behaviour; R for regulating access to the behaviour; and E for empowerment, which corresponds precisely to the *raison d'être* of the treatment of addiction. "Treatment is empowerment because it makes it easier to engage in the new behaviour by normalising the physiological functioning or creating the conditions in which it can normalise."

2. Main points to retain from the seven thematic sessions of the conference

Session 1 – Advances in research in the neurobiology of addictions: what is new in the development of more efficacious treatments?

This first session – addressed by five speakers – made it possible to confirm the undeniable vitality of this area of research, which is concerned with identifying and analysing at the molecular level the brain mechanisms brought into play by the consumption of drugs and the systemic effects of repeated or chronic consumption on neural functioning.

This vitality is clearly manifested at the conceptual level, as illustrated by the first two contributions by Jean-Pol Tassin (Collège de France) and Pier Vincenzo Piazza (INSERM – Bordeaux). Starting from different assumptions, these two scientists and their respective teams concurred in calling into question the dopaminergic paradigm, which constitutes the traditional reference framework for addiction neuroscience research. According to this paradigm, all the drugs that induce dependence trigger the release of dopamine in various structures of the brain, stimulating the brain's reward pathways and producing pleasure. Dependence then naturally comes about as the user repeats the drug intake in order to achieve this pleasure all the time. Jean-Pol Tassin's work suggests that the search for pleasure is not a sufficient condition for addiction, as the dopaminergic system activated by taking the drug is in fact regulated by two upstream neurotransmission systems: the serotoninergic system and the noradrenergic system. Working on this basis, a number of experiments conducted on animal models have made it possible to demonstrate that repeated drug-taking result in the decoupling of these two systems, which are normally linked to, and mutually regulate, one another. This decoupling has two consequences: it induces a state of tension, impulsivity and palpable malaise among the animals stimulated by the drug and it triggers the compulsive repeat intake of drugs, which probably enables the two systems temporarily to link up once again and thus brings about a temporary respite.

For their part, Pier Vincenzo Piazza and his team said they had been interested for 10 years in the key question of the variability of individual responses to drugs and, consequently, in the differences that exist regarding the risk of becoming dependent. Various experiments conducted on animal models clearly showed that not all the animals exposed to heavy drug consumption became dependent, that is they did not succumb to unbridled consumption with a loss of control and continued use despite its harmful consequences (electric shocks). Only 15-17 % of the animals exposed to the drug would go on to develop addictive behaviour, which was a percentage very close to that observed in humans. Chronic exposure to drugs could thus not be considered sufficient to cause addiction. On the basis of these findings, which call into question the dopaminergic paradigm (the pleasure procured by the drug is not enough to induce dependence), Pier Vincenzo Piazza and his team have set out to identify and analyse the neuronal factors of the variability of individual responses to drugs. Two independent phenotypes seem to be responsible for the development of drug addiction. The first, which is correlated to a strong reactivity to stress, anxiety and impulsivity, increases the appetite for more drugs and facilitates the chronic intake of large doses of toxins. This research team has collected a substantial amount of data showing that this vulnerability is due to an increase in the activity of glucocorticoid hormones and dopaminergic neurons of the mesencephalon. However, real drug addiction – compulsive drug-taking with a loss of control – only develops in a limited number of subjects who possess a second phenotype that is "vulnerable to addiction". At the moment, Pier Vincenzo Piazza wishes to direct his research towards identifying the biological bases of this second phenotype, about which virtually nothing is known today. Their discovery could open up some completely new paths with regard to the treatment of addiction.

The vitality of addiction neurobiology can also be seen in neuropharmacological research, and this was illustrated by the next contribution by Rainer Spanagel (Central Institute of Mental Health, Heidelberg University, Germany) on the prevention of relapses among alcohol-dependent individuals. He pointed out that recent research in this field had enabled numerous neuromediator systems to be identified as being involved in cravings and relapses among alcoholics: opioidergic, glutamatergic and endocannabinoid systems, the signalling mechanism being triggered by corticoliberine (CRF). The use of animal models specifically designed to develop and evaluate medication treatments for the prevention of alcohol relapses enabled the role played by those systems in alcohol addiction and relapses to be demonstrated. For example, it was by confirming the clinical effectiveness of naloxone and acamprosate, two molecules that act on the opioidergic and glutamatergic systems, that animal models had made it possible to confirm the hypothesis that those two systems played an important role in alcohol dependence. Those experimental data were revealing new targets of therapeutic interest, and clinical trials with their ligands were under way.

The last two presentations of this session (by Jean-Luc Martinot, INSERM-CEA, Orsay, and Günter Schumann, Institute of Psychiatry, King's College, London) illustrated the potential of research into the medical imaging of addictions, which benefits from the spectacular progress recorded in imaging techniques in the last few years. This progress has opened up new areas of research for neurobiologists that enable them to build extremely promising bridges between fundamental hypotheses (at the biological, genetic or anatomical level) and observations of the brain (functional neuroanatomy *in vivo*) in animals (preclinical neuroimaging) and humans (clinical neuroimaging) in experimental drug use situations. In this connection, Günter Schumann gave a description of the European integrated project IMAGEN, in which he is involved with Jean-Luc Martinot's team. The aim of the project was to study behaviour reinforcement mechanisms among normal subjects and under pathological conditions. This was a multi-centre research programme that combined genetic studies and neuroimaging on a cohort of 2 000 14 year-olds. The risk phenotypes for mental disorders and/or addiction were investigated on the basis of clinical, behavioural, cognitive and neuroimaging data.

Session 2 – What approaches for treating addictions to cocaine and crack?

The aim of this second session of the conference was to provide an update on the most recent data on the different treatment options currently being explored by researchers and clinicians to deal with addiction to cocaine and crack and to assess their future potential: immunotherapy, other pharmacological approaches, psychosocial approaches. There is no validated treatment protocol that has provided documented evidence of its effectiveness in terms of maintaining abstinence in the case of this rapidly growing form of addiction. It is known that the chronic use of cocaine is accompanied by health and behaviour risks that, far from being harmless, are being increasingly documented in the scientific literature. Furthermore, the rapid spread of the use of this powerful psychostimulant in different social strata is also reflected by the occurrence of social damage that adversely affects both other individuals and society as a whole, such as the commission of acts of violence (including sex attacks) under the influence of a feeling of personal supremacy provided by the product, and road or other accidents resulting from this feeling and from an underestimation of the risks it entails.

The first contribution in this session was on the immunotherapy or "anti-cocaine" vaccine solution. The speaker, Professor Thomas Kosten of the Baylor College of Medicine in Houston, Texas, is the world's leading specialist in this area of research. He pointed out that the principle of the anti-drug vaccine consisted in synthesising antibodies with the ability to lower drug concentrations in the various brain structures (after consumption) by neutralising them before the blood-brain barrier is crossed. This effect resulted from the molecular size of the antibodies, which prevented either the antibody or the antibody/drug complex from entering the brain. He and his team had been working for more than 10 years on the production of antibodies resulting from the chemical coupling of the drug with a toxin, such as the cholera toxin. The clinical trials recently conducted by this research team had shown that the vaccine developed was really effective, with a vaccine response rate of about 70-75 %. The post-vaccination latency time was two to three months before obtaining the peak of neutralising activity. The prediction of a good response could be improved by taking account of the subject's genetic factors, and an increase in the immune response could be obtained by co-administering cytokines or more effective adjuvants than those traditionally used. The precise role that this method could play in the treatment of people dependent on cocaine (treatment of overdoses, relapse prevention, other?) and the ethical principles governing its use remained to be determined.

The second speaker, Dr Xavier Castells (Faculty of Medicine, Autonomous University of Barcelona, Spain), mentioned the state of the research under way on identifying substitution treatments that can be effective in the case of cocaine dependence. He pointed out that a large variety of medical drugs containing antidepressants, antipsychotics, dopaminergic agonists or thymo-regulators had been tested to treat cocaine dependence, but none had proved to be clearly effective. To date, there was therefore no medication with official approval for the treatment of cocaine dependence, whether it be from the European Medicines Agency (EMEA) or its American equivalent (the FDA). The "substitution treatment" approach was different from that taken in the aforementioned work: the aim was to identify medical drugs with a mechanism of action and effects similar to cocaine (namely, the stimulation of the central nervous system), but with less addictive potential and capable both of avoiding craving and withdrawal syndrome and of leading ultimately to abstinence. In that context, substitution treatments based on dextroamphetamine, mazindol, methylphenidate, modafinil and bupropion had been evaluated during controlled clinical trials. Encouraging results had been obtained and further research was needed, especially in the case of dextroamphetamine and bupropion.

The third contribution (by Dr Pier Paolo Pani) concerned a recent meta-analysis carried out in the context of the Cochrane reviews relating to the effectiveness of antipsychotics-based treatments for cocaine addiction. Antipsychotic drugs had been used for this because of their ability to block the dopamine receptors and counterbalance the peaks of dopaminergic activity brought about by taking cocaine. The meta-analysis had related to three antipsychotic molecules: risperidone, olanzapine and haloperidol. The summary of the results of the clinical trials studied did not reveal tangible effectiveness of those three antipsychotic drugs in the indication of the treatment of cocaine dependence. Cocaine dependence was still a disorder for which no effective drug was available, but the neurobiological knowledge accumulated on the subject should ultimately lead to new drug-based approaches.

The last contribution (by Dr Laurent Karila, Department of Psychiatry and Addiction, Paul Brousse Hospital, Villejuif, France) discussed behavioural approaches in the treatment of cocaine-dependent individuals and pointed out that cocaine dependence was a complex, heterogeneous and multifaceted disorder. Three types of behavioural approach for treating drug-dependent individuals had been gradually developed over the past three decades: cognitive-behavioural therapies (development of the ability to cope and to prevent relapses), contingency management approaches (abstinence incentives in the form of shopping vouchers, approaches based on progressively higher financial rewards) and approaches involving the strengthening of social ties (interventions based on a combination of different behavioural therapy techniques).

All those psychosocial treatments were intended to improve patient compliance and encourage abstinence, and several groups were working on the adaptation of those behavioural therapies to the specific aspects of cocaine addiction. No data were currently available in the literature that enabled it to be argued that one or other of those approaches contributed to the prevention of relapses (which remained the key aspect of the care provided), even though contingency management could lay claim to producing encouraging results in the English-speaking countries, where it was beginning to come into general use. In the years to come, the best working basis was no doubt a mixed approach that combined behavioural therapies with treatment of a pharmacological nature.

Session 3 – The contributions of community-based approaches

Although the development of therapeutic communities (TCs) for the treatment of drug users has been relatively limited in France, worldwide they constitute one of the main approaches for the long-term care of drug addicts. In view of the importance gained by this method of residential care, it was essential to schedule a whole conference session on this subject.

Over the last 30 years, several authors have looked into the matter of the therapeutic effectiveness of TCs. This is particularly difficult given the diverse nature of the TCs, the heterogeneous composition of the group of people accommodated there and the frequent lack of information on what has become of patients since they left. Having said that, all the evaluations carried out between the early 1980s and the end of the 1990s agree on the fact that the most constant success factor is the duration of the care and assistance, whatever the underlying treatment model.

Since these different activities have not succeeded in identifying a standard profile of patients for whom the treatment is more likely to succeed (especially with regard to maintaining long-term abstinence), no clear answer has so far been provided to the question of whether the effectiveness of the TCs depends on the duration of residents' stay in the community facility or, conversely, on their predisposition to remain in treatment.

The two presentations scheduled for this third session focused on revisiting this question in the light of the most recent research.

The first contribution (by Dr Eric Broekaert, Department of Orthopedagogics, Ghent University, Belgium) provided an analysis of the development of TCs for drug users in Europe centred on the influence exerted by the traditional TC (American and Canadian) model on European TCs. The facilities set up in Europe between the late 1960s and the early 1990s had initially been very strongly influenced by the American model, which was characterised by a rejection of methadone treatments for opiate dependents and of purely psychiatric approaches to addiction. Subsequently, the European supporters of TCs had altered this initial model by restoring the role of doctors in the treatment plan and emphasising the techniques of social rehabilitation (social learning). Instead of exclusively focusing on behaviourism, European TCs laid more stress on dialogue and understanding, and health professionals now played a role that was at least as important as that played by former users.

The aim of the second contribution (by Dr Lesley Smith, School of Health and Social Care, Oxford Brookes University, Oxford) was to report on a Cochrane review recently carried out on the evaluation of the effectiveness of therapeutic communities and of other forms of residential treatment for drug users. After a bibliographical search in the international databases, two authors had independently selected the studies for inclusion, by assessing their quality and extracting the relevant data. Wherever possible, the data had been presented in a quantitative format with reference to relative risks (RR) and the differences between averages. In the other cases, the results had been subjected to a qualitative analysis.

Seven studies had been chosen. The differences between them had ruled out any pooling of data, and the results for each had been recapitulated individually. No study had really argued that TCs offered therapeutic added value in comparison with other forms of residential treatment. Similarly, it was difficult to conclude that one type of TC was more efficient than another. However, it was pointed out that in institutional environments there was an advantage in providing TCs rather than nothing at all or simply mental health treatment programmes with the aim of preventing relapses. However, since the methodological limitations of the studies could result in skewed results, Dr Smith believed it was not possible to draw a firm conclusion on the benefits of TCs.

Session 4 – What is the medium and long-term outcome for patients receiving opiate substitution treatments?

Opiate substitution treatments based on prescribed methadone have been administered for over 40 years in the United States and have developed in a very large number of countries. France was late in introducing them (1995-96), but their use spread particularly rapidly.

In all the countries in which they have been introduced, substitution treatments have made possible substantial improvements in the state of health and general situation of street heroin users, even though undesirable consequences of certain treatment methods have been observed (misuse of high-dose buprenorphine, in particular). This improvement was first documented in a series of cross-cutting studies, but longitudinal cohort studies were very quickly set up in several countries, for example the DARP study in the United States performed from 1969 onwards, then the TOPS (1979) and DATOS (1991) studies, the NTORS study in the United Kingdom (1995), the MANIF study in France (1995) centred on a cohort of intravenous drug users infected by the Aids virus, and the VEdeTTE study in Italy (1997).

The main feature of this fourth session of the conference was that it brought together as speakers people responsible for the three major European cohort studies that are today producing monitoring and evaluation data on the best

57

opiate substitution treatments. The subjects dealt with illustrate the diversity of the areas covered by these three studies, whether they involve health-related aspects (lessening of the additional risk of death, better patient compliance in respect of associated diseases) or behavioural and social aspects (reduction in criminal offences and convictions).

The first contribution (by Professor Michael Gossop, National Addiction Centre, King's College, London) concerned an aspect normally little explored in the evaluation of substitution treatments: changes in social behaviour among users undergoing these treatments. Professor Gossop pointed out that the five-year monitoring of users in the NTORS cohort had revealed a significant reduction in a large number of areas in the difficulties normally linked to the problematic behaviour of drug users. That included a reduction in the use of illegal drugs and in injections and syringe sharing, as well as in criminal behaviour associated with the acquisition of street drugs. Whereas high levels of criminal conduct had been observed prior to the start of the treatment of the individuals in the NTORS study, there had been a significant drop in the number of offences recorded afterwards, and the reduction had been maintained during the five-year monitoring period. Crime associated with drug acquisition and the use and sale of drugs had gone down by almost a quarter, and an analysis of convictions entered in the judicial records confirmed that drop in criminal offences. Multivariate analyses of the data had confirmed the assumption that the drop in criminal behaviour was largely due to the reduction in regular and/or addictive use of street heroin. Professor Gossop stressed that the reduction in crime following substitution treatment was of considerable practical importance, as it meant that the treatments brought society substantial and immediate benefits in terms of a drop in the economic costs of crime. However, they were also a source of considerable, albeit less tangible advantages for the victims because of the reduction in the psychological damage inflicted on them.

The second contribution (by Ms Patricia Schifano, Department of Epidemiology of the Local Health Authority, Rome, Italy) concerned the influence of substitution and other specialised treatments on overdose-induced mortality rates of users. The work on which she reported is based on the VEdeTTE prospective cohort study involving 10 454 heroin users in treatment in Italy between 1998 and 2001, equivalent to 10 208 persons/year in treatment and 2 914 persons/year out of treatment. With regard to estimating the mortality rate, the analysis presented was based on the standardised mortality ratio (SMR), which is an estimate of the higher risk of death for heroin users in and out of treatment compared with the general population. The Cox model also used compares the overdose risk ratio between heroin users in and out of treatment.

Ms Schifano pointed out that, after taking account of confounding variables, whatever the type of treatment undergone by the subjects of the cohort study, protection against death from an overdose was still a significant factor compared with the risk of death when out of treatment. The study also revealed a very high risk of a lethal overdose in the month following release from or interruption of the treatment. This fact underlined the strategic importance of better health education for drug users and the introduction of relapse prevention programmes and programmes to prevent death by overdose in the end-of-treatment period.

The final contribution (by Ms Patrizia Carrieri, INSERM – Marseille) focused on what is an important issue given the number of HIV-infected intravenous drug users: the impact of substitution treatments using methadone or high-dose buprenorphine on patient compliance with antiretroviral HIV treatments. On the basis of the MANIF cohort, longitudinal data on compliance with HIV treatments and on the symptoms reported in connection with this treatment, as well as on substitution treatments and risk-taking following the first pre-scription of HIV treatment, had been collected among HIV-infected drug users receiving HIV treatment in different hospital departments. The patients included had been classified on the basis of the substitution treatment received and according to whether they continued to inject. The patients who had received no substitution treatment and had not injected any drugs during the period studied had been considered abstinent and had served as a reference category. A logistic regression model based on a generalised evaluation equa-tion had been used to study the influence of methadone or buprenorphine and continuous injecting on non-compliance with HIV treatment and to investigate the impact of methadone or buprenorphine on the symptoms reported in connection with this treatment.

After making an adjustment for the consumption of alcohol, depression and secondary effects, the study had clearly showed that the compliance of "abstinent" patients and patients on substitution treatment who had stopped injecting was comparable to that for HIV treatment. On the other hand, the risk of non-compliance among substituted or unsubstituted patients continu-ing to inject was two and three times higher respectively than among abstinent patients. Furthermore, there was a significant link between the time spent on substitution without injecting and virological success.

Session 5 – What treatment options for young problematic users of cannabis?

Since the early 1980s, there has been a considerable increase in cannabis consumption among teenagers and young adults in all developed countries. This increase can be seen at all stages of the use of this illegal drug: experi-mentation, occasional use, regular use and daily use. As in the case of cocaine addiction, there is at the moment no internationally validated protocol for the treatment of young heavy cannabis users. However, encouraging results were published in the scientific literature of the early 2000s by a team of American clinicians who had implemented a family-based treatment (Multi-Dimensional Family Therapy, or MDFT), which they had adapted to the specific problem of cannabis use.

This fifth session of the conference focused on the presentation of a study designed to assess the clinical effectiveness of the MDFT model in the organisational and clinical context of five European countries: France, Germany, the Netherlands, Belgium and Switzerland. Two speakers involved in this study (Dr Olivier Phan, Medical Officer at Centre Emergence-Tolbiac, Paris, and Dr Andreas Gantner, Director of the Therapieladen Centre, Berlin, Germany) set out to describe this multi-centre clinical trial, known as the INCANT (International Need for CANnabis Treatment) study.

Dr Phan pointed out that the MDFT method was a family-based therapy of systemic origin. It included a number of variables such as the teenager's personality, the family, the environment and the interactions between those variables. The therapy was carried out in three stages: the construction of the foundations of the treatment process, the demand for changes and, finally, the consolidation of the progress made, the main idea being to have a direct impact on the risk and protection factors in order to bring consumption to an end.

The protocol drawn up for the INCANT study, common to the teams of the five participating countries, provided for the MDFT model and its measurable effects to be compared to the TAU (Therapy As Usual) and the French TAUe (Therapy As Usual *explicitée*) model. In France, the TAU model generally consisted of three stages: the therapeutic alliance, assistance for the patient to evaluate his or her own consumption, and work on the themes specific to adolescence. Dr Gantner described the German TAU, pointing out that it was an individual non-manualised therapy consisting of motivational interviews and cognitive behavioural therapy.

Ultimately, the main assessment criterion for this longitudinal and comparative evaluation of clinical methods was the reduction in the consumption of cannabis among teenagers included in the study who abused and/or were dependent on that substance.

In December 2008, 336 patients had been included in Europe, 96 of them in Germany and 76 in France. The provisional results suggested that the MDFT was potentially more effective than the TAU and TAUe models.

The discussion that followed this very stimulating presentation enabled the participants to exchange views on the benefits and potential of, and the difficulties in transposing, therapeutic models in the specific area of providing treatment for addicted teenagers.

Session 6 – Change without treatment: interest and possibilities

Pioneering research work carried out in the 1960s and 1970s clearly showed that individuals who had abused or been dependent on drugs for a long time had managed to change their behaviour and either control or halt their consumption without having recourse to medical or professional help. This work opened up a new avenue of research on a hitherto little studied phenomenon, namely "spontaneous discontinuation" or, more aptly, "behavioural changes or discontinuation without treatment".

At the moment, whereas the question of behavioural changes without treatment is leading to an important line of research at international level, it is being virtually ignored in France. This research theme lays out a new paradigm of addiction, which is understood neither as social deviance (the traditional perspective of American normative psychosociology) nor as a chronic disorder (the current paradigm of addictology) but as the permanent bringing into play of the free will of the subject. This redefinition will result in new questions being asked by everyone involved in addiction research.

Given these issues, it was the wish of those responsible for organising the conference to hold a specific session on this subject that would enable recent work undertaken by European teams in this original line of research to be described and discussed.

The first speaker (Dr Harald Klingemann, Director of the Swiss consortium for research on the treatment, Sedhang, Switzerland) set out to provide an overview of the concept of self-change, with all the problems of definition and the methodological difficulties raised by this concept. He pointed out that many addicts changed their behaviour on their own, so the systems for specialised treatment of addictions only reached approximately 25 % of the groups concerned.

Referring to the data on self-change in the literature on the subject since the 1970s, Mr Klingemann drew attention to what he regarded as the five key questions that still needed to be analysed more closely so that this area of research could really make a contribution to improving care in the field of addiction medicine:

– Can self-change be observed more frequently among certain specific drug-user profiles (conceptual problems)?

– Do they belong to particular social networks (heterogeneity of these users)?

– What link is there between self-change processes and risk-reduction measures (possible support for self-change)?

– Does the stigmatisation associated with addiction treatment reduce a person's motivation to seek professional help and does it consequently encourage individuals to shy away from specialised care (obstacle to entering treatment)?

– How can addiction medicine professionals observe and gain insights into the self-change process (raising the awareness of therapists and lessons to be drawn for clinical practice)?

The second speaker in this session (Dr Hans-Jürgen Rumpf, Research Group on Substance Abuse, Lübeck University, Germany) reported on his research work on the ability of individuals to stay alcohol-free after breaking their dependence at the end of a self-change process and, accordingly, without recourse to formal medical or professional help.

Dr Rumpf said it was now generally accepted that overcoming alcohol dependence through self-change was the main path by which people broke with this form of addiction. However, some authors had suggested that success was short-lived and lacked stability. In order to analyse this question in greater depth, he had set up a 24-month monitoring study involving a cohort of former drinkers who had succeeded in becoming abstinent by themselves. The participants had been recruited by means of advertisements in the media and through a general population survey. At the beginning, all the participants (n = 114) had met the criterion of having broken with alcohol dependence in the 12 months preceding the survey without previously undergoing formal treatment (namely, a situation of complete remission from alcohol dependence according to the DSM-IV criteria, the sample excluding two self-help groups and anyone who had undergone outpatient or residential treatment).

Towards the end of the monitoring period, four persons had died; the other subjects had been re-interviewed (that is, 92.9 %). Of the latter, 92.3 % were still in remission from their alcohol dependence without professional help, 1.5 % were once again alcohol dependent according to the DSM-IV criteria, 1.5 % were also considered alcohol dependent on the basis of related information, 1.5 % met one or two dependence criteria and 4.6 % were availing themselves of professional help. The survey clearly suggested that self-remission from alcoholism was not a transient phenomenon for the vast majority of people concerned. That, incidentally, was why the study of former drinkers who had succeeded in achieving abstinence by themselves was able to produce valid information on paths out of dependence.

The last contribution in this session (Professor José Luis Carballo, Chair of Psychology, Miguel Hernández University, Elche, Spain) concerned one of Harald Klingemann's five questions, namely what can distinguish patients who seek formal help in freeing themselves from their addiction from those who take action to do so by themselves? The protocol set up in this connection comprised two samples of Spanish drug users, one group having undergone treatment to free themselves from their dependence and the other having managed to do this on their own. The aim of the study had been to evaluate, in a different sociocultural context from that of the author's previous investigations (populations in English-speaking countries), the possible differences between the two groups in terms of a series of variables linked to lifestyle changes and the maintenance of abstinence.

Thus, 58 former users of illegal drugs or alcohol who for at least a year had been having difficulties in remaining abstinent had been recruited by means of advertisements in the media. Out of that total, 29 had weaned themselves off their addiction and 29 had done so with the help of treatment. All of them had been assessed during individual interviews on their addiction and their success in breaking with it, and had been subsequently compared with regard to those aspects. The results had shown that the two groups were basically similar, although important and substantial differences had been found with regard to the intensity of the dependence, psychiatric comorbidity, polytoxicomania and the strategies employed to maintain abstinence. The study accordingly suggested that addiction profiles were surely more pronounced among drug users who had followed a treatment programme than in the other group. However, that result was not constant in other studies.

Session 7 – How can we better organise addiction treatment research at the European level?

The situation of addiction and treatment path research is very mixed. On the one hand, this is a dynamic area of research with numerous teams from different disciplines (life science, epidemiology and public health, human and social sciences) producing a significant stream of works and publications. On the other hand, it is an area of research that remains relatively fragmented owing to the compartmentalisation of individual disciplines, national boundaries, the highly scattered nature of sources of funding and support – all of them characteristics that can only impede the advancement of knowledge. The fact is that the health and social issues involved in the consumption of drugs remain considerable, whether we are thinking in terms of premature death, morbidity or, indeed, social damage.

Against this background, the principal aim of the round table organised for this final session of the conference was to take stock of the difficulties faced in the field of addiction research and to open up realistic prospects for improving the visibility, structuring and funding of this area.

The round table brought together representatives of the European Commission (Directorates General of Research, Health and Justice), the European Monitoring Centre for Drugs and Drug Addiction (EMCDDA), the Research Platform of the Council of Europe's Pompidou Group, the French ministers of research and health, and the French National Institute for Health and Medical Research (INSERM).

The discussions were preceded by three introductory presentations: by Caroline Hager (DG Justice) on the organisation of drug research bodies in the 27 EU countries, by Roland Simon (EMCDDA) on the state of drug research in the 27 EU countries and by Florence Mabileau-Whomsley (Council of Europe Pompidou Group) on the presentation of the online register of current drug research in the various Council of Europe countries, which is a very interesting initiative that owes much to the spirit of innovation that traditionally guides the work of the Pompidou Group's Research Platform.

In the ensuing discussions, several paths were outlined: pooling of some research capabilities, encouragement to draw up interdisciplinary projects and/or set up European clinical projects, involvement of the pharmaceutical industry, dissemination of collective techniques such as brain imaging, and the maintenance of significant underlying pure research – especially in the field of the addiction neurosciences – the dynamic nature of which must be preserved.

Programme of the European Conference of Scientific Experts (9 and 10 December 2008)

"How can we treat drug addiction better? New scientific and clinical challenges for Europe"

Languages of presentations: French, English and German with simultaneous interpretation

Day 1: Tuesday 9 December 2008

8 a.m.-9 a.m. Welcoming coffee, distribution of badges and conference materials

> *9 a.m.-10.30 a.m. Opening session*

– Introduction by the President of the MILDT, Etienne Apaire

– Speech by the Director of INSERM, Gérard Breart

– Speech by the minister for health, Mrs Roselyne Bachelot

– Presentation of the objectives and structure of the conference: What does it mean to treat addictions? – Robert West (editor-in-chief of *Addiction* journal, London, United Kingdom)

10.30 a.m.-11 a.m. Coffee break with "poster session"

> *11 a.m.-1 p.m. Session 1 – Advances in research into the neurobiology of addictions: what is new in the development of more effective treatments? Chairperson and moderator: Michel Hamon (Paris, France)*

Communications

– Proposal for a new neurobiological model for drug addiction: Jean-Pol Tassin (Paris, France)

– Relative weight of drug exposure and individual vulnerability in the development of addiction: Pier Vincenzo Piazza (Bordeaux, France)

– Drugs for relapse prevention in alcoholism; 10 years of progress: Rainer Spanagel (Mannheim, Germany)

– Imaging common addictions: tobacco, cannabis and alcohol: Jean-Luc Martinot (Orsay, France) and Gunter Schumann (London, United Kingdom)

2.30 p.m.-4.30 p.m. Session 2 – Which approaches for treating addiction to cocaine and crack?
Chairperson and moderator: Jean-Michel Scherrmann (Paris, France)

Communications

–   Anti-addiction vaccines: Thomas Kosten (Houston, USA)

–   Substitution treatment with CNS stimulants for cocaine dependence: Xavier Castells (Barcelona, Spain)

–   Antipsychotic medications for cocaine dependence: Pier Paolo Pani (Cagliari, Italy)

–   Behavioural therapies for the treatment of cocaine dependence: Laurent Karila (Villejuif, France)

4.30 p.m.-5 p.m. Coffee break and "poster session"

5 p.m.-6 p.m. Session 3 – The potential of community-type approaches
Chairperson and moderator: Joël Swendsen (Bordeaux, France)

Communications

–   The development of therapeutic communities for addictions in Europe: Eric Broekaert (Ghent, Belgium)

–   Therapeutic communities for substance-related disorders: Lesley A. Smith (Oxford, United Kingdom)

–   State and quality of treatment in Europe for drug users, presentation of the report by the Directorate General Health and Consumers of the European Commission: Natacha Grenier (DG SANCO C4, Luxembourg)

6.30 p.m. Cocktail

Day 2: Wednesday 10 December 2008

9 a.m.-11 a.m. Session 4 – What are the medium and long-term outcomes for patients receiving opiate substitution treatments?
Chairperson and moderator: Yolande Obadia (Marseille, France)

Communications

–   Reductions in criminal convictions following addiction treatment: 5 years follow-up: Michael Gossop (London, United Kingdom)

–   Risk of fatal overdose during and after specialist drug treatment: the VEdeTTE study, a national multi-site prospective cohort study: Patrizia Schifano (Rome, Italy)

–   Benefits of treatments for opioid dependence in HIV-infected patients: results from the MANIF 2000 cohort: Patrizia Carrieri (Marseille, France)

11 a.m.-11.30 a.m. Coffee break and "poster session"

11.30 a.m.-1 p.m. Session 5 – What treatment options are there for young people who are problem cannabis users?
Chairperson and moderator: Michel Reynaud (Villejuif, France)

Communication

–   Presentation of the research protocol for the European clinical multi-site INCANT study and initial data: Olivier Phan (Paris, France) and Andreas Gantner (Berlin, Germany)

2 p.m.-3.30 p.m. Session 6 – Quitting without treatment: the potential benefits
Chairperson and moderator: Philippe Batel (Clichy, France)

Communications

–   Self-change from addictive behaviours: a new perspective: Harald Klingemann (Südhang, Switzerland)

–   Stability of remission from alcohol dependence without formal help after two years: Hans-Jürgen Rumpf (Lübeck, Germany)

–   Differences among substance abusers in Spain who recovered with treatment or on their own: José Luis Carballo (Elche, Spain)

3.30 p.m.-4 p.m. Coffee break and "poster session"

4 p.m.-5.50 p.m. Session 7 – How can we better organise addiction treatment research at the European level? (round table)
Chairperson and moderator: Frédéric Rouillon (Paris, France)

–   Presentation of the first results of the report ordered by the Directorate General Justice, Freedom and Security of the European Commission on the organisation of drug research in the 27 countries of the Union: Caroline Hager (DG Justice, Brussels)

–   Presentation of the summary report established by the European Monitoring Centre for Drugs and Drug Addiction (EMCDDA) on the state of drug research in the European Union: Roland Simon (EMCDDA, Lisbon)

–   Presentation of the online registry of ongoing research on drugs in the different countries of the Council of Europe: Florence Mabileau-Whomsley (Pompidou Group of the Council of Europe, Strasbourg)

Expected participants in the round table: Jacques Demotes-Mainard (ministry of higher education and research), a representative (ministry of health, youth, sports and associations), Jean-Antoine Girault (INSERM), Natacha Grenier (DG SANCO – European Commission), Caroline Hager (DG Justice – European Commission), Richard Muscat (Pompidou Group Research Platform

– Council of Europe), Roland Simon (EMCDDA), a representative (DG Research – European Commission)

6 p.m.-6.30 p.m. Closing discourse by the minister of higher education and research, Mrs Valérie Pecresse

Pompidou Group publications and documents

Publications[3]

2007 ESPAD Report: *Substance use among students in 35 European countries*, by Hibell, Björn; Guttormsson, Ulf; Ahlström, Salme; Balakireva, Olga; Bjarnason, Thoroddur; Kokkevi, Anna; Kraus, Ludwig; the Swedish Council for Information on Alcohol and Other Drugs (CAN); the European Monitoring Centre for Drugs and Drug Addiction (EMCDDA) and the Council of Europe Co-operation Group to Combat Drug Abuse and Illicit Trafficking in Drugs (Pompidou Group) [ISBN 978-91-7278-219-8], February 2009. Can be ordered directly from the Swedish Council for Information on Alcohol and Other Drugs (CAN), tel.: + 46 8 412 46 00, fax: + 46 8 10 46 41, e-mail: can@can. se, www.can.se

Attention deficit/hyperkinetic disorders: diagnosis and treatment with stimulants, proceedings of seminar, Strasbourg, December 1999 [ISBN 92-871-4240-8]

Connecting research, policy and practice – Lessons learned, challenges ahead – Proceedings [ISBN 92-871-5535-6]

Contribution to the sensible use of benzodiazepines, proceedings of seminar, Strasbourg, January 2001 [ISBN 92-871-4751-5]

Development and improvement of substitution programmes, proceedings of seminar, Strasbourg, October 2001 [ISBN 92-871-4807-4]

Drug addiction, (2005), Ethical Eye Series, Council of Europe Publishing [ISBN 92-871-5639-5], July 2005

Drug-misusing offenders and the criminal justice system, proceedings of seminar, Strasbourg, October 1998 [ISBN 91-871-3790-0]

Drug-misusing offenders in prison and after release, proceedings, seminar, Strasbourg, October 1999 [ISBN 92-871-4242-4]

Hartnoll, Richard, *Drugs and drug dependence: linking research, policy and practice – Lessons learned, challenges ahead*, background paper, Strategic Conference, Strasbourg, 6-7 April 2004 [ISBN 92-871-5490-2]

Kopp, Pierre, *Calculating the social cost of illicit drugs: methods and tools for estimating the social cost of the use of psychotropic substances* [ISBN 92-871-4734-5], November 2001 (available in Russian, December 2003)

---

3. Council of Europe "publications" are ISBN books available for purchase. "Documents", however, are available for free and do not have an ISBN.

Leopold, Beate and Steffan, Elfriede, *Special needs of children of drug misusers*, Consultants' final report [ISBN 92-871-3489-8], 1997

Muscat, Richard, *Drug use in prison*, project of the Group of experts in epidemiology of drug problems: final report by co-ordinator [ISBN 92-871-4521-0], December 2000

Muscat, Richard (2006), *Biomedical research in the drugs field* [ISBN 978-92-871-6017-1], July 2006

Muscat, Richard, Bjarnasson, Thóroddur, Beck, François and Peretti-Watel, Patrick (2007), *Risk factors in adolescent drug use: evidence from school surveys and application in policy* [ISBN 978-92-871-6196-3], February 2007

Muscat, Richard, *From a policy on illegal drugs to a policy on psychoactive substances*, in collaboration with members of the Pompidou Group Research Platform [ISBN 978-92-871-6480-3], Strasbourg, January 2009

Negreiros, Jorge (2006), *Psychological drug research: current themes and future developments* [ISBN 978-92-871-6032-4], September 2006

Outreach, proceedings of symposium, Bergen, February 1993 [ISBN 92-871-2601-1]

Pregnancy and drug misuse, proceedings of symposium, Strasbourg, March 1997 [ISBN 92-871-3784-6]

Pregnancy and drug misuse: Update 2000, proceedings of seminar, Strasbourg, May 2000 [ISBN 92-871-4503-2]

Prisons, drugs and society, proceedings of seminar, Bern (Switzerland), September 2001 [ISBN 92-871-5090-7]

Rhodes, Tim, *Outreach work with drug users: principles and practice*, consultant's final report [ISBN 92-871-3110-4], 1996

Risk reduction linked to substances other than by injection, proceedings of seminar, Strasbourg, February 2002 [ISBN 92-871-5329-9]

Road traffic and drugs, proceedings of seminar, Strasbourg, April 1999 [ISBN 92-871-4145-2]

Road traffic and psychoactive substances, proceedings of seminar, Strasbourg, 18-20 June 2003 [ISBN 92-871-5503-8], published July 2004

"Le rôle de la recherche scientifique dans l'élaboration des politiques de drogue" (2008), Séminaire international en co-opération avec l'Office National de Lutte contre la Drogue et la Toxicomanie d'Algérie, Algiers, 3-6 December 2006, proceedings published May 2008 (only in French and Arabic)

Sinclair, Hamish (2006), *Drug treatment demand data – Influence on policy and practice* [ISBN 978-92-871-6086-7], October 2006

Vocational rehabilitation for drug users in Europe, proceedings of seminar, Bratislava, January 2000 [ISBN 92-871-4406-0]

Women and drugs, proceedings of symposium, Prague, November 1993 [ISBN 92-871-2838-3]

Women and drugs – Focus on prevention, proceedings of symposium, Bonn, October 1995 [ISBN 92-871-3508-8]

Documents[4]

Böllinger, Lorenz, "The general potential of police prevention in the area of illicit drugs" [P-PG/Prev (2003) 2], September 2003

"Drug testing at school and in the workplace and appendices" [P-PG/Ethics (2008) 5], September 2008

"Ethics and drug use – Seminar on ethics, professional standards and drug addiction, Strasbourg, 6-7 February 2003" [P-PG/Ethics (2003) 4], November 2003

"European handbook on prevention: alcohol, drugs and tobacco" (1998)

Hedrich, Dagmar, "Problem drug use by women – Focus on community-based interventions" [P-PG/Treatment (2000) 3]

Korf, Dirk J. et al., "Drugs and alcohol: violence and insecurity? Guide – Integrated project 2 – Responses to violence in everyday life in a democratic society" [P-PG/CJ (2004) 7], September 2005

"La prise en charge des toxicomanes", séminaires de formation de médecins dans la cadre du projet MedNET en Algérie, 1st semester 2008, proceedings, by the Office National de Lutte Contre la Drogue et la Toxicomanie (Algérie), (only in French and Arabic), December 2008

Moyle, Paul, "International drug court developments: models and effectiveness" [P-PG/DrugCourts (2003) 3], September 2003

"New signals for drug policies across Europe", ministerial conference, Strasbourg, 27-28 November 2006 [P-PG/MinConf (2007) 1], proceedings, June 2007

"Prisons, drugs and society: a consensus statement on principles, policies and practices" – published by WHO (Regional Office for Europe) in partnership with the Pompidou Group, September 2002

Stillwell, Gary and Fountain, Jane, "Benzodiazepine use: a report of a survey of benzodiazepine consumption in the member countries of the Pompidou Group" [P-PG/Benzo (2002) 1], February 2002

---

4. Without ISBN, with P-PG reference.

Svensson, Njål Petter, "Outreach work with young people, young drug users and young people at risk – Emphasis on secondary prevention" [P-PG/Prev (2003) 6], September 2003

"Targeted drug prevention – How to reach young people in the community?" report of the conference in Helsinki, November 2002

Uchtenhagen, Ambros, Schaaf, Susanne and Berger, Christa, "Vocational rehabilitation of drug users and drug dependent persons (EUREHA Project)", report on the state of the art and on the results of a survey in all member states of the Pompidou Group (Addiction Research Institute at Zurich University) [P-PG/ Rehab (2000) 1]

Wijngaart, G.F. van de and Leenders, F., "Working group on 'Minorities and drug misuse', consultants' final report" [P-PG/Minorities (98) 1] 1998

To order P-PG documents:

Council of Europe
Pompidou Group – Documentation
Catherine Lahmek
F-67075 Strasbourg Cedex
France

tel.: + 33 (0)3 88 41 29 87/fax: + 33 (0)3 88 41 27 85
e-mail: pompidou.group@coe.int
www.coe.int/pompidou

To order paying publications with ISBN online:
http://book.coe.int

Sales agents for publications of the Council of Europe
Agents de vente des publications du Conseil de l'Europe

BELGIUM/BELGIQUE
La Librairie Européenne -
The European Bookshop
Rue de l'Orme, 1
BE-1040 BRUXELLES
Tel.: +32 (0)2 231 04 35
Fax: +32 (0)2 735 08 60
E-mail: order@libeurop.be
http://www.libeurop.be

Jean De Lannoy/DL Services
Avenue du Roi 202 Koningslaan
BE-1190 BRUXELLES
Tel.: +32 (0)2 538 43 08
Fax: +32 (0)2 538 08 41
E-mail: jean.de.lannoy@dl-servi.com
http://www.jean-de-lannoy.be

BOSNIA AND HERZEGOVINA/
BOSNIE-HERZÉGOVINE
Robert's Plus d.o.o.
Marka Maruliça 2/V
BA-71000, SARAJEVO
Tel.: + 387 33 640 818
Fax: + 387 33 640 818
E-mail: robertsplus@bih.net.ba

CANADA
Renouf Publishing Co. Ltd.
1-5369 Canotek Road
CA-OTTAWA, Ontario K1J 9J3
Tel.: +1 613 745 2665
Fax: +1 613 745 7660
Toll-Free Tel.: (866) 767-6766
E-mail: order.dept@renoufbooks.com
http://www.renoufbooks.com

CROATIA/CROATIE
Robert's Plus d.o.o.
Marasoviçeva 67
HR-21000, SPLIT
Tel.: + 385 21 315 800, 801, 802, 803
Fax: + 385 21 315 804
E-mail: robertsplus@robertsplus.hr

CZECH REPUBLIC/
RÉPUBLIQUE TCHÈQUE
Suweco CZ, s.r.o.
Klecakova 347
CZ-180 21 PRAHA 9
Tel.: +420 2 424 59 204
Fax: +420 2 848 21 646
E-mail: import@suweco.cz
http://www.suweco.cz

DENMARK/DANEMARK
GAD
Vimmelskaftet 32
DK-1161 KØBENHAVN K
Tel.: +45 77 66 60 00
Fax: +45 77 66 60 01
E-mail: gad@gad.dk
http://www.gad.dk

FINLAND/FINLANDE
Akateeminen Kirjakauppa
PO Box 128
Keskuskatu 1
FI-00100 HELSINKI
Tel.: +358 (0)9 121 4430
Fax: +358 (0)9 121 4242
E-mail: akatilaus@akateeminen.com
http://www.akateeminen.com

FRANCE
La Documentation française
(diffusion/distribution France entière)
124, rue Henri Barbusse
FR-93308 AUBERVILLIERS CEDEX
Tél.: +33 (0)1 40 15 70 00
Fax: +33 (0)1 40 15 68 00
E-mail: commande@ladocumentationfrancaise.fr
http://www.ladocumentationfrancaise.fr

Librairie Kléber
1 rue des Francs Bourgeois
FR-67000 STRASBOURG
Tel.: +33 (0)3 88 15 78 88
Fax: +33 (0)3 88 15 78 80
E-mail: librairie-kleber@coe.int
http://www.librairie-kleber.com

GERMANY/ALLEMAGNE
AUSTRIA/AUTRICHE
UNO Verlag GmbH
August-Bebel-Allee 6
DE-53175 BONN
Tel.: +49 (0)228 94 90 20
Fax: +49 (0)228 94 90 222
E-mail: bestellung@uno-verlag.de
http://www.uno-verlag.de

GREECE/GRÈCE
Librairie Kauffmann s.a.
Stadiou 28
GR-105 64 ATHINAI
Tel.: +30 210 32 55 321
Fax.: +30 210 32 30 320
E-mail: ord@otenet.gr
http://www.kauffmann.gr

HUNGARY/HONGRIE
Euro Info Service
Pannónia u. 58.
PF. 1039
HU-1136 BUDAPEST
Tel.: +36 1 329 2170
Fax: +36 1 349 2053
E-mail: euroinfo@euroinfo.hu
http://www.euroinfo.hu

ITALY/ITALIE
Licosa SpA
Via Duca di Calabria, 1/1
IT-50125 FIRENZE
Tel.: +39 0556 483215
Fax: +39 0556 41257
E-mail: licosa@licosa.com
http://www.licosa.com

MEXICO/MEXIQUE
Mundi-Prensa México, S.A. De C.V.
Río Pánuco, 141 Delegacíon Cuauhtémoc
MX-06500 MÉXICO, D.F.
Tel.: +52 (01)55 55 33 56 58
Fax: +52 (01)55 55 14 67 99
E-mail: mundiprensa@mundiprensa.com.mx
http://www.mundiprensa.com.mx

NETHERLANDS/PAYS-BAS
Roodveldt Import BV
Nieuwe Hemweg 50
NE-1013 CX AMSTERDAM
Tel.: + 31 20 622 8035
Fax.: + 31 20 625 5493
Website: www.publidis.org
Email: orders@publidis.org

NORWAY/NORVÈGE
Akademika
Postboks 84 Blindern
NO-0314 OSLO
Tel.: +47 2 218 8100
Fax: +47 2 218 8103
E-mail: support@akademika.no
http://www.akademika.no

POLAND/POLOGNE
Ars Polona JSC
25 Obroncow Street
PL-03-933 WARSZAWA
Tel.: +48 (0)22 509 86 00
Fax: +48 (0)22 509 86 10
E-mail: arspolona@arspolona.com.pl
http://www.arspolona.com.pl

PORTUGAL
Livraria Portugal
(Dias & Andrade, Lda.)
Rua do Carmo, 70
PT-1200-094 LISBOA
Tel.: +351 21 347 42 82 / 85
Fax: +351 21 347 02 64
E-mail: info@livrariaportugal.pt
http://www.livrariaportugal.pt

RUSSIAN FEDERATION/
FÉDÉRATION DE RUSSIE
Ves Mir
17b, Butlerova ul.
RU-101000 MOSCOW
Tel.: +7 495 739 0971
Fax: +7 495 739 0971
E-mail: orders@vesmirbooks.ru
http://www.vesmirbooks.ru

SPAIN/ESPAGNE
Mundi-Prensa Libros, s.a.
Castelló, 37
ES-28001 MADRID
Tel.: +34 914 36 37 00
Fax: +34 915 75 39 98
E-mail: libreria@mundiprensa.es
http://www.mundiprensa.com

SWITZERLAND/SUISSE
Planetis Sàrl
16 chemin des Pins
CH-1273 ARZIER
Tel.: +41 22 366 51 77
Fax: +41 22 366 51 78
E-mail: info@planetis.ch

UNITED KINGDOM/ROYAUME-UNI
The Stationery Office Ltd
PO Box 29
GB-NORWICH NR3 1GN
Tel.: +44 (0)870 600 5522
Fax: +44 (0)870 600 5533
E-mail: book.enquiries@tso.co.uk
http://www.tsoshop.co.uk

UNITED STATES and CANADA/
ÉTATS-UNIS et CANADA
Manhattan Publishing Co
2036 Albany Post Road
USA-10520 CROTON ON HUDSON, NY
Tel.: +1 914 271 5194
Fax: +1 914 271 5886
E-mail: coe@manhattanpublishing.coe
http://www.manhattanpublishing.com

Council of Europe Publishing/Editions du Conseil de l'Europe
FR-67075 STRASBOURG Cedex
Tel.: +33 (0)3 88 41 25 81 – Fax: +33 (0)3 88 41 39 10 – E-mail: publishing@coe.int – Website: http://book.coe.int

CuRIOSITIES AT MEDWAY LIBRARY